The Journal of Montaigne's Travels in Italy: In Italy by Way of Switzerland and Germany

Michel de Montaigne, William George Waters

BIBLIOLIFE

THE JOURNAL OF
MONTAIGNE'S TRAVELS
IN ITALY BY WAY OF SWITZER-
LAND AND GERMANY
IN 1580 AND 1581

TRANSLATED AND EDITED

WITH AN INTRODUCTION AND NOTES

By W. G. WATERS

AUTHOR OF "JEROME CARDAN," ETC.

IN THREE VOLUMES

VOL. II

LONDON
JOHN MURRAY, ALBEMARLE STREET
1903

CONTENTS

LIST OF ILLUSTRATIONS
VOL. II

THE JOURNAL OF
MONTAIGNE'S TRAVELS
IN ITALY

V

ITALY

VERONA is about the size of Poitiers, having a vast quay beside the Adisse, which flows through it and is crossed by three bridges. I went thither also with the baggage. Without the bulletins of health, which had been issued at Trante and confirmed at Rovere, our party would not have been admitted within the town; not that there was any talk of danger of the plague, but this is always done by custom or by way of tricking wayfarers out of a few coins. We went to the cathedral, where M. de Mon-

A

taigne remarked on the strange behaviour
of those present at High Mass on such a
solemn day.   They chattered in the very
choir of the church, standing with their hats
on, and turning their backs to the altar, and
recking naught of the office except at the
time of elevation.   There were an organ and
violins, which gave musical accompaniment
to the mass.   We visited other churches, but
saw nothing noteworthy, either in the ornaments or in the beauty of the women present.
Amongst others we went to the church of
Saint George, where the Germans have left
divers marks of their presence and several
coats-of-arms, together with an inscription
relating how certain German noblemen in the
train of the Emperor Maximilian, what time
he came to take Verona from the Venetians,
placed a certain piece of work over one of
the altars.   M. de Montaigne remarked that
the government here preserved the memory
of its reverses, as it also preserved in their
integrity the beautiful tombs of the ill-starred
Scaligers.   It is a fact that our host of the

VERONA

"Chevalet," an excellent house, where we found a superfluity of good fare and a bill one-fourth more than we would have paid in France, enjoyed the privilege of burying his family in one of the tombs aforesaid. We also visited, under the guidance of the castellan's lieutenant, the castle where the government keeps on foot sixty soldiers; more, as M. de Montaigne was informed, as a safeguard against the townsfolk than against foreign foes; and then went to a religious house occupied by Jesuates de Saint Jerosme. These are not priests, neither do they say mass or preach, being for the most part ignorant, but they are skilful distillers of citron and other sorts of water, both here and in other places. They wear white frocks, small white caps, and over this a cloak of dark russet, and are very fine young men. Their church is excellently appointed, as is also their refectory, in which supper was already laid.

We saw likewise some very ancient masonry of the Roman period which is said to be an

remains to be done before it will be in its ancient state,[1] and it is doubtful whether the whole efforts of the city will be able to accomplish this rebuilding. The place is oval in shape, and contains forty-three rows of seats, each a foot or rather more in height, the measure of the circumference at the highest point being some six hundred paces.[2] The gentlefolk of the country still use it for jousting and other public games.

M. de Montaigne also saw somewhat of the Jews, having visited their synagogue and held long converse concerning their ceremonies. The city has many fine squares and market-places, and from the castle, which stands on high ground, we could discern

[1] Coryat, who saw it in 1608, describes it as greatly ruined and put to base uses. Much of the marble had been taken away to other buildings ; but the damage was being repaired by the Veronese noblemen, who had already spent sixty-six thousand crowns over the restoration. To build it in England, he estimates, would cost two million pounds.

[2] Modern measurements are 502 feet by 401, and 98 feet high.

Mantua, which lay some twenty miles distant to the right of our road. Here there is no want of inscriptions, seeing that they never renew a gutter, either in the towns or along the highways, without inscribing thereupon the names of the Podestà and of the artificer. Like the Germans they nearly all use some armorial device, traders as well as others. In Germany indeed, not only the towns, but also the larger portion of the villages lay claim to exhibit their coats-of-arms.

We quitted Verona, and on our way out of the city we saw the church of Our Lady of Miracles,[1] famous by reason of certain marvellous things which have there come to pass. On account of these manifestations, the church has been rebuilt after a beautiful circular design. Some of the bell-towers are covered with brickwork laid crosswise. We traversed a flat country of varied character, fertile here and barren there, the

[1] Madonna di Campagna, one of the finest works of Sammicheli.

mountains on our left hand being far distant, with some on the right also, and rode thirty miles in one stretch to Vicenza where we supped.

This is a handsome town, somewhat smaller than Verona, and full of noblemen's palaces.[1] On the morrow we visited several churches and saw the fair, which was at that time being held in the great square, many shops having been built of wood especially for the occasion.[2] We also visited the house of the Jesuates, which is a very handsome one, and saw their store of distilled water, for the public sale of which they keep a shop. We bought two bottles of scent for a crown. They make likewise medicinal draughts for all sorts of maladies. The founder of this

[1] Palladio had died a short time before Montaigne's visit, *i.e.* August 19, 1580. Vicenza was at this time at the height of its beauty, all the noteworthy buildings, except the Teatro Olimpico, having been completed.

[2] The fairs of Vicenza were amongst the largest in Italy, and were instituted in the thirteenth century. During their continuance all the shops in the city had to be closed. Fairs were held up to the middle of the present century.

order was P. Urb. S. Jan Colombin,[1] a noble
of Siena, who made the foundation in 1367,
and it is at present under the protection of
the Cardinal de Peluco. They have thirty
monasteries, all of which are in Italy, and
their house here is a very beautiful one. It
is said they scourge themselves every day,
and they keep little chains in their cells,
where they pray without singing, and for
a certain time during the day they meet
together.

At this place we failed to get old wine,
which troubled me greatly on account of
M. de Montaigne's colic; for he had to drink
thick wine instead of the good wine we had
got up to this time. We thought of the

---

[1] The founder was the chief magistrate of the city, and
is said to have been moved to religious enthusiasm by
reading the life of S. Mary of Egypt. Montaigne is
wrong in giving 1367 as the date of the foundation of
the order; it was the year of Colombini's death. The
members of the order were originally laymen, and chiefly
occupied in preparing drugs. Urban V. placed them
under the Augustinian rule. In 1606 they were allowed
to be ordained, and in 1660 were suppressed by
Clement IX.

German wines with regret, though they are for the most part spiced and diverse in their odour, and though they have a liquorish flavour like sage; indeed, they call one of them *vin de sauge*, which is pleasant enough when the palate is wonted thereto, seeing that it is also good and generous. We set out from this place on the Thursday after dinner by a road very level, wide, straight, ditched on both sides and slightly raised above the plain. On either hand the country was very fertile, and the mountains, as before, were in the far distance. After a journey of eighteen miles we reached Padua in time for bed.

Here the hostelries can in no respect be compared with those of Germany. Certes they are less costly by one-third, and resemble those of France. The city is goodly, wide in extent, and in my opinion holds within its bounds an area at least as big as that of Bordeaux; but the streets are narrow and ugly, lacking both in people and in seemly dwellings. Its situation is very pleasant, in an open plain stretching wide on every side. We tarried here all the following day and saw the schools of fencing, dancing, and equitation,[1] at which more than a hundred French gentlemen were at this time seeking instruction. M. de Montaigne deemed that it worked greatly to the detriment of these young countrymen of ours that they should thus live together and still practise the customs and language of their native land, letting go the chance of making acquaintance with strangers. He was vastly pleased with the church of St. Antony, the cupola of which is not constructed whole in itself, but of several sections made into the form of a dome; the church likewise contains much rare sculpture work in marble and bronze. M. de Montaigne saw with much pleasure the portrait bust of Cardinal Bembo,[2] which

[1] It is singular that Montaigne makes no mention of the University. Italy was then the great school of fencing, as he notices in the *Essais*, ii. 27.

[2] Coryat notices this bust, and gives the inscription written by Paolo Giovio: "Petri Bembi Cardinalis

bears all the marks of a refined character and an indefinable something testifying to the gracefulness of his intellect. The hall where justice is dispensed is the largest unsupported by pillars I ever saw, and at one end thereof is the head of Titus Livius, figuring him an emaciated man of a studious

imaginem Hieronymus Quirinus Ismerii filius in publico ponendam curavit: ut cujus ingenii monumenta æterna sint, ejus corporis quoque memoria ne a posteris desideretur. Vixit annos 76, M. 7, D. 29. Obiit 15 Calend. Februarii anno 1547." Writing of the other tombs Coryat says: "Amongst others in the Cloyster I observed one that made me even lament, the monument of a certaine English Nobleman, namely, Edward Courtney, Earle of Devonshire, who was buried here in the time of Queen Mary; he died there in his youth, and was the sonne of Henry, Earle of Devonshire and Marquesse of Exceter, who was beheaded in the time of King Henry the Eighth. This Edward Courtney was afterward restored by Queen Mary. Truely it strooke great compassion and remorse in me to see an Englishman so ignobly buried, for his body lieth in a poore woodden Coffin placed upon another faire monument, having neither epitaph nor any other thing to preserve it from oblivion, so that I could not have knowne it for an Englishman's Coffen, except an English gentleman, Mr. George Rooke, had told me of it."—*Crudities* (1776), vol. i. p. 176.

and melancholy temper.[1]   This is an ancient
work of which naught is known save by
tradition.   His epitaph is there also, having
been set, as was its due, in a place of honour
after its discovery.   Over one of the doors
of this palace is a figure of Paul the jurisconsult,[2] but this M. de Montaigne pronounced to be a modern work.   A house
standing on the site of the ancient arena in
a garden is worth a visit.

Students can live here cheaply at seven
crowns a month for the master and six for
the servant in respectable boarding-houses.

[1] Coryat says: "He is represented according to his
olde age : for his face is made very leane and shaved."
The inscription under it, "Ve T. Livius Liviæ I. F.
Quartæl. Halys concordialis Patavi sibi et suis omnibus,"
has probably no reference to Livy at all. It was discovered in 1363 near the church of San Giustina and
removed to the Sala della Ragione. This is the one
which Montaigne mistakes for Livy's epitaph. Another
inscription records the gift of Livy's arm-bone to Alfonso
the Magnanimous in 1450. Coryat mentions a second
statue of Livy, made of freestone, and says that this was
the effigy brought, together with an inscription underneath, "from Saint Gustinae's Church." The monument
at the end of the hall was erected in 1547.

[2] Julius Paulus, who wrote in the time of Alexander
Severus.

We left early on the Saturday morning, traversing a very fine road beside the river, and having on either hand fields very fertile with corn, and well shaded by rows of trees, upon which the vines were trained. All along the road fine pleasure houses had been built, and over the gate of one of these belonging to the Contarini is an inscription telling how the king[1] lodged here on his way back from Poland. After travelling twenty miles we stopped for dinner at Chaffousine,[2] which is naught but an inn, and here we took boat for Venice. Here they bring ashore all the boats with machinery and pulleys worked by two horses after the fashion of an oil mill. They move their boats by means of

[1] Henry III. He fled secretly from Cracow on hearing of the death of Charles IX. in 1574, but once clear of Poland he was in no hurry to get back to France. He spent two months in traversing Lombardy, and was regaled sumptuously by all the petty princes and nobles. The Emperor Maximilian and the Doge of Venice gave him much excellent advice, but he was only impressed by the processions and dances and fine dresses, which he proposed to reproduce in France.

[2] Fusina.

wheels placed underneath, which run along planks and thereby convey them over to the canal which runs into the sea on which Venice is situated. We took dinner at Chaffousine, and, having embarked in a gondola, arrived at Venice in time for supper after travelling five miles.

On the morning of the morrow, Sunday, M. de Montaigne saw M. de Ferrier,[1] the king's ambassador, who welcomed him heartily and took him to Mass and back to his house to dinner. On the Monday he and M. d'Estissac again dined there.

[1] Arnaud du Ferrier was a distinguished French jurisconsult. Henry IL made him President of the Chambre des Enquêtes. He represented France at the Council of Trent, and by a violent anti-Roman speech he raised a great uproar and was sent as ambassador to Venice in quasi disgrace, and there Montaigne met him. According to Brantôme he used to repair to Padua and there lecture on law. The king was greatly displeased at this and recalled him. Henry of Navarre invited him to his court and he became a Protestant. He died in 1585.

On the margin of the MS. Montaigne has written : "Ce viellard, qui a passé septante cinq ans, à ce qu'il dit, jouit d'un eage sein & enjoué. Ses façons & ses discours ont, je ne sçay quoi de scholastique, peu de vivacité et de pouinte. Ses opinions panchent fort evidamment, en matiere de nos affaires, vers les innovations Calviniennes."

One remark let fall by the ambassador amongst divers others seemed to him very strange, to wit, that he (the ambassador) held no conversation with the people of the city, who were of a humour so suspicious that should one of their number speak to him only twice, this one would be looked upon askance.[1]   M. de Ferrier also informed him that the city of Venice brought an annual income of fifteen hundred thousand crowns to the Signory.[2]   With regard to the curi-

[1] A decree of the Council of Ten, July 12, 1380, ordains : "Si quis nobilis vel civis acciperet literas ab aliquo de extra de re spectante ad statum nostrum, illas capitibus Consilii tenerentur subito presentare, et Capita debeant inquirere diligenter principium talis praticæ, ut nostri cives omnino starent separati ab omni pratica et commercio dominorum et comunitatum, et ab omni pratica rei spectantis ad statum."

[2] Fynes Moryson writes (Part iv., ed. 1903, p. 128): "I find the generall Revenue of this State valued at two millions of gold yearly, though Monsr. Villamont attributes so much to the citty of Venice alone . . . and for particular cittyes these relations record, that Padoa brings yearly into the Treasure of Venice thirteene thousand Ducates ; Vicenza thirtye two thousand ; Verona nyntye thousand ; Brescia (besydes many extraordinary Subsidyes) one hundred thousand four hundred and fyfty ; Bergamo fyfty thousand ; Vdane twenty fyve thousand ;

osities of the place they are familiar enough,
and M. de Montaigne said that he had
found Venice different from what he had
anticipated, and that, after he had made a
diligent visitation of the city, he was somewhat disappointed. The government, the
situation, the arsenal, the Place of St. Mark,
and the vast crowds of foreigners, seemed to
him most worthy of remark of anything he
saw. On Monday November, 6, while he sat
at supper, the Signora Veronica Franca,[1] a

Trevigi fourskore thousand." But farther on he says :
"A late writer hath published in print that the generall
Revenue of Venice amounts yearely to two millions of gold
crowns : that the Townes yield yearely eight hundred
thousand Crownes."—A great disparity. Montaigne probably refers to the share of Venice alone.

[1] There is a life of this lady by Tassini—*Veronica
Franco celebre letterata e meretrice venesiana.* She was
married in her youth to one Paniza, a physician, but she
left him to take up the career of a courtesan. Her name
appears in that extraordinary document which the late
Earl of Orford printed for private circulation in 1870 :
"Catalogo di tutte le principal et piu honorate Corte-
giane di Venetia, il nome loro, et il nome delle loro
pieze, et le stantie ove loro habitano, et di piu ancor vi
narra la contrata ove sono le loro stantie, et etiam il
numero de li dinari che hanno da pagar quelli gentil
homini, et al che desiderano entrar nella sua gratia."
Her description runs : " 204, Veronica Franca, a Santa

noble Venetian lady, sent for his acceptance
a little book of letters which she had put
together, whereupon he gave two crowns to
the bearer.   On the Tuesday after dinner he
had an attack of colic which lasted two or
three hours; it was not, as far as could be
seen, one of his worst, and before supper
he passed two large stones, one after the
other.   He failed to perceive in the women
of Venice that great beauty for which they

Maria Formosa, pieza so mare 2 scudi." In 1574 she
gave up her profession, and by her wit and beauty
gained a status not unlike that of her forerunners in
Athens. She certainly enjoyed the friendship of divers
men of note, Domenico and Marco Veniero, Marcantonio
della Torre and Tintoretto. Henry III. visited her
when passing through Venice and took away her portrait. In middle life she devoted herself to religion and
good works, and tried to induce the Signoria to found
an asylum for penitent women. She died in 1591, aged
forty-five. The book she sent to Montaigne was probably *Lettere famigliari a diversi*, dedicated to Cardinal Luigi d'Este. Lord Orford evidently had not read
Tassini's book or Montaigne's *Voyage*, otherwise he
would have been able to give a more precise date to the
Catalogo, which he puts down vaguely to the sixteenth
century. According to Fynes Moryson, "the tribute to
the State from the Cortizans was thought to exceede
three hundreth thousand Crownes yearely."

are famed. He saw some of the highest class of those who make a market of their charms, and this institution appeared to him more marvellous than any other of the city, to see such a vast number of them, some hundred and fifty, spending money like princesses over furniture and attire, with no other source of income than the traffic aforesaid. Again, divers of the nobles of the city entertained courtesans at their own charges in the sight of every one. M. de Montaigne hired for his use a gondola for day and night as well at a charge of two livres, about seventeen sous, with no extra expenditure for the boatman. Provisions are as dear here as in Paris, but it is the cheapest town in the world for living, for a train of servants is here quite useless, and every one goes about unattended. The cost of apparel is in like degree moderate; moreover, no one has occasion for a horse. On Saturday the twelfth of November we left and returned to Chaffousine, a distance of five miles, and here we and our servants

VENICE

and baggage got on board a boat, for which
we paid two crowns. M. de Montaigne
was somewhat in fear of water transit, being
advised that it deranged his stomach;[1] and

[1] " Il me semble avoir veu en Plutarque rendant la
cause du souslevement d'estomach, qui advient à ceux
qui voyagent en mer, que cela leur arrive de crainte :
après avoir trouvé quelque raison, par laquelle il prouvé,
que la crainte peut produire un tel effet. Moy qui y suis
fort sujet, sçay bien, que cette cause ne me touche pas.
Et le sçay, non par argument mais par nécessaire ex-
périence. Sans alleguer ce qu'on m'a dit, qu'il en arrive
de mesme souvent aux bestes, specialement aux porceaux
hors de toute apprehension de danger. . . . Or je ne puis
souffrir longtemps ny coche, ny littière, ny bateau, et
hay toute autre voiture que de cheval. Mais je puis
souffrir la lictière moins qu'un coche; et par même raison
plus aisément une agitation rude sur l'eau, d'où se produit
la peur, que le mouvement qui se sent en temps calme.
Par cette legère secousse, que les avirons donnent, des-
robant le vaisseau sous nous, je me sens brouiller, je ne
sçay comment, la teste et l'estomach : comme je ne puis
souffrir sous moi un siège tremblant. Quand la voile ou
le cours de l'eau, nous emporte esgalimêt, ou qu'on nous
rouë, cette agitation unie, ne me blesse aucunement.
C'est un remuëment interrompu, qui m'offence : et plus,
quand il est languissant. Je ne sçaurois autrement
peindre sa forme. Les medecins m'ont ordonné de me
presser et sangler d'une serviette le bas du ventre, pour
remedier à cet accident : ce que je n'ay point essayé,
ayant accoustumé de lucter les defauts qui sont en moy,
et les dompter par moy-mesme."—*Essais*, iii. 6.

now, being minded to ascertain whether the motion on this river, which indeed is most steady and uniform provided that the boat be drawn by horses, would cause him inconvenience, he made trial of it and found that he suffered no ill effects therefrom. On this channel we had to pass one or two lock gates which open and shut to the passers-by. After a voyage of twenty miles by water we reached Padua in time for bed.

M. de Caselis here parted company with us and tarried in Padua on a pension of seven crowns a month for good food and lodging. He might have taken his valet for five crowns; the pensions here are of the highest class and frequented by the best of company, for instance the Sieur de Millan, son of M. de Salignac. As a rule the guests have no servants of their own, but are served by the valet of the house, or by women. Each guest has an excellent room, and finds his own fuel and light; the catering, as we had reason to know, being very good. Living in this manner is exceedingly cheap,

and this in my opinion is the reason why so
many strangers who are no longer students
resort hither. It is not the custom to ride
through the streets or to be attended by
servants. In Germany we noted that all
men down to the hand workers carried
swords, a practice not adopted in this
country. After dinner on Sunday, November 12, we went to see the baths to the
right of the city, going to Abano[1] direct.
This is a small village at the very foot of
the mountains. Three or four hundred
paces beyond it is a rocky plateau, somewhat higher than the ground adjacent, and
on this elevation, which is of considerable
extent, several springs of hot water issue
from the rocks, which water cannot be used
at the source for the bath—and much less
for drinking—on account of its great heat.
Wherever it runs it leaves a grey trace like

[1] These baths were famous in Roman times—*Fons
Aponus*. Livy, Valerius Flaccus, and Pietro d'Abano,
the great mediæval physician, were born here. The
baths have been restored, and are now crowded in the
season.

burnt cinder and a heavy deposit which
resembles petrified sponge, its taste being
salt and sulphurous. Indeed the whole
region is perfumed thereby, for the brooks,
which run in all directions over the level
ground, convey to a great distance the heat
and the smell aforesaid.

Two or three small houses, ill enough
furnished, serve the needs of the patients,
the water being brought to the baths in
the houses by channels from the springs.
Exhalations rise not only from the water
itself, but also from every crack and crevice
of the rocks, which give out heat everywhere, so that the people there have dug
out certain places in which a man may lie
down and get the heat of the exhalations
and fall into a sweat. M. de Montaigne
took a little of the water in his mouth,
after it had lost its excessive heat by
standing awhile, and found it tasted more
of salt than of anything else.

Furthermore to the right of this place
we perceived the abbey of Praie, noted for

its wealth, its beauty, and its liberal and courteous reception of strangers. M. de Montaigne would not go there, having settled with himself that it behoved him to revisit all these parts, and especially Venice, at his leisure, and that this present visit was as nothing.[1] He had simply gone to see Venice, attracted by the exceedingly great renown of the city, and affirmed that he would tarry neither at Rome nor elsewhere in Italy without having paid another visit to Venice. Reckoning on this event, he left at Padua, in charge of M. François Bourges, a Frenchman, the works of Cardinal Cusan[2] which he had purchased in Venice. From Abano we went to a place called S. Pietro,[3]

[1] This statement helps to account for the curious brevity of Montaigne's stay in Venice. The abbey in question is Praglia, a Benedictine house of great repute for its wealth and liberality.

[2] Nicola di Cusa, a learned mathematician, a German by birth. His work deals chiefly with statics, or rather with the weight of bodies in water. He also put forth an ingenious hypothesis as to the motion of the earth. His works were published at Basel in 1565.

[3] San Pietro Montagnon, a bath still in use. There is another San Pietro in Bagno near Cesena.

lying low, and as we went we had the
mountains close to us on our right hand.
This is a land of meadows and pasturage,
but the air is thick in certain spots with
the vapour of the hot springs, some boil-
ing hot and some lukewarm: some springs
indeed are quite cold. The taste is somewhat flatter and more insipid than that of
the other springs, and there is less of the
odour of sulphur and the taste of salt. We
came upon some traces of ancient buildings,
and two or three mean hovels for the
lodging of guests; but in truth the place
is very barbarous, and I would be sorry to
send thither any friend of mine. The report is that the Signiory sets little store by
such places, and looks askance at the prospect of an influx thither of gentlefolk from
foreign parts. M. de Montaigne said that
these last-named baths reminded him of
those of Preissac[1] near to Aix. The water

[1] Probably Prèchac, a bath much frequented, lying
near Dax in Navarre. Munster, *Cosmog.*, i. 375, com-
mends the baths of this region.

thereof leaves a reddish trace, and a deposit like mud on the tongue. He could detect no special taste, and fancied it was charged with iron.

On our departure from this place we passed a very fine house belonging to a Paduan gentleman, where M. le Cardinal d'Este [1] was then sojourning. He was sick with gout and had been there more than two months for the sake of the baths, but more on account of the near vicinity of the ladies of Venice and all sorts of diversion. Thence we travelled eight miles to Bataille,[2] where we arrived in time for bed. This is a small village on the canal of Fraichine [3] which, having not more than two or three feet of water, is navigated by boats of a very strange fashion. There we were served on earthen dishes and on plates

[1] Luigi d'Este, brother of Alfonso II. of Ferrara. He was one of Tasso's earliest patrons, and took him to Paris in 1570. He was only in deacon's orders, and, from Montaigne's remarks, was evidently a free liver. In 1561 he was made cardinal, and died in 1586.

[2] Battaglia, about five miles beyond Abano.

[3] Frassine, a canalised river, which joins the Fratta and runs parallel with the Adige to the sea.

of wood and not of pewter, but otherwise we
did not fare badly. On the Monday morning
I myself[1] went on ahead with the mule while
the others visited the baths[2] situated some
five hundred paces distant along the bank
of the canal. From M. de Montaigne's
description, they found there only one bath-
house, with ten or twelve chambers. In May
and August a number of visitors come, but
these for the most part lodge in the village
or in the castle of Seigneur Pic, where also
lodged M. le Cardinal d'Este. The bath-
water comes down from a small mountain
ridge, and runs through channels into the
houses below. The patients do not drink
thereof but rather of the water of S. Pierre[3]
which is fetched for them. The water in its
descent from the ridge runs beside other

[1] The secretary.
[2] The baths of S. Elena. They were probably known
to the Romans, but their modern use dates from the
middle of the fifteenth century, when they were brought
to notice by Giov. Dondi. Later on, in the seventeenth
century, Il Dottore Selvatico restored the bath-houses, and
greatly increased the repute of the place.
[3] San Pietro Montagnon, near Abano.

channels of good sweet water, and it is hotter
or colder in ratio to the length of its course.
M. de Montaigne was for investigating the
source up above, but no one could point it
out to him, and indeed it appeared that it
had a subterraneous origin. He found that
it left little taste in the mouth, like that of
S. Pierre, and that it was scarcely sulphurous
or salt at all; moreover, that its effect when
drunk would resemble that of the water
aforesaid. In the bath-house there are other
chambers where the water only comes in by
drops under which any affected member is
placed, and they told M. de Montaigne that
the forehead was the part most often treated
for ailments of the head. At certain points
on these channels small cabins of stone have
been constructed, to which the patients may
repair, and having opened the hole communicating with the channel, they quickly
fall into a sweat through the exhalations and
heat of the water. There are also rooms for
dry heat, made in various fashions, but mud
baths are what they chiefly use. This

treatment is practised in a large bath below
the bath-house and open to the sky, fitted
with a machine by which the mud is pumped
up to the house adjacent. Here are provided
divers appliances of wood made to fit each
limb—legs, arms, thighs and other parts—
wherein the member to be treated is placed
and the appliance filled with mud, which is
renewed as often as is needed. This mud is
as black as that of Barbotan, but less full of
grains and more greasy, moderately hot and
quite odourless. The nearness to Venice is
the only advantage which any of these baths
possesses, all the surroundings being gross
and unrefined. Near this spot we[1] came to
the bridge over the canal which is known as
the Canal of the Two Thoroughfares, which
pass both below and above it. Here they
have constructed causeways, which on the outside are on a level with the roads along which
the traffic passes, and on the inside slope down

[1] The secretary seems to have been still absent at this
point, as the narrative is written in the third person, but
for the sake of coherence it seems better to keep to
the first.

to the level of the waterway.   Here is built
a stone bridge of two arches over which the
canal is carried, and above this bridge is built
another from one bank to the other, for
the service of those who may want to cross
the canal, and under it go the boats which
traverse the waterway.   Here also descends
from the mountains a large stream, which,
after flowing through the plain, crosses the
course of the canal; and it was to compass
this passage without any interruption to the
navigation that the first-named two-arched
bridge was constructed.   The stream, which
itself is of volume sufficient to float small
boats, here passes under the canal, its sides
being faced with wooden planks.   So that,
reckoning this stream, and the canal itself,
and the bridge crossing the same, there are
three routes in use one over the other.

From hence onwards, the canal being left
on the right hand, the road passed by a small
town called Montselise which, though it lies
very low, was enclosed by a wall carried almost to the top of the mountain.   Within

this wall stood an ancient castle belonging
to the former lords of the place and now a
heap of ruins.   At this point, leaving the
mountains to the right, we kept to the left
along a fine level raised road, which at certain seasons of the year must be well shaded.
On either side lay a very fertile plain, the
several cornfields thereof being thickly planted
with rows of trees from which hung the vines,
as is the usage in this country.   Hereabout
so many great grey oxen are seen that their
presence did not cause in us the surprise we
had felt at the sight of those belonging to the
Archduke Fernand.

We found ourselves now upon a high bank
made beside the river, with marshes on either
side more than fifteen miles in extent, and
as wide as the eye could compass.   In other
days there were extensive swamps which the
Signiory attempted to drain and bring under
cultivation.   In some places success has been
achieved, but in very few.   At present the
view is over a muddy sterile country, thick
set with cane growth, the attempt to change

its character having resulted in loss rather
than gain. We crossed the Adisse[1] on a
floating bridge which was placed on two
small boats, and was capable of carrying
fifteen or twenty horses; passing over by a
rope fastened to a point some five hundred
paces distant in the water. To keep this
rope aloft several small boats are stationed
here and there and fitted with forked poles
which hold up the long cord. After a
journey of twenty-five miles we arrived in
time for bed at Rovigo, a small town belonging to the Signiory aforesaid. Here they
gave us salt in lumps, which the people take
as if it were sugar. There is as great abundance of provision here as in France, in spite
of what has been said to the contrary. They
do not lard their roast meat, but the savour
thereof is not much affected by this omission.
The chambers in the matter of glass windows
and shutters are inferior to our own, but the
beds are better made and smoother, with an
abundant supply of mattresses. They are

[1] Adige.

fitted, however, almost always with small ill-fashioned canopies, and the supply of white sheets is meagre. Of these, indeed, a solitary traveller, or one with mean equipage, would most likely go lacking altogether. Charges were the same, or perhaps a trifle higher than in France. In this town was born the good Celius, surnamed *Rodoginus*.[1] It is a very handsome place with a fine square, and the river Adisse flowing through it.

On the morning of Tuesday, November 15, we departed, and after going some long distance along a causeway like the one at Blois, we crossed, first the Adisse and then the Po on floating bridges like that of the day antecedent, save that on the bridges last-named are cabins where they take payment for the transit according to the printed and prescribed regulations, and, moreover, stop the raft in the middle of the stream to do their reckoning and exact payment from all passengers before suffering them to land. After disembarking on a low-lying plain, over which the

[1] Luigi Ricchieri, one of the first of the Humanists.

road must be impassable in rainy weather, we journeyed in one spell to Ferrara, arriving there at eventide, after travelling twenty miles.

Here on account of the Manifest and bill of health we were kept a long time at the gate, a delay which had also happened to us at other places. The city is about the size of Tours and lies in a very level country. The palaces are numerous; the greater part of the streets are wide and straight and very scantily peopled. On the Wednesday morning M. de Montaigne and M. d'Estissac went to kiss the duke's[1] hands; their intention having been made known to him, he sent a gentleman of the court to receive them and conduct them into his cabinet, where he was with two or three others. We went through several private chambers, in which we saw divers well-dressed gentlemen, and then entered the duke's presence. We found

[1] Alfonso II., son of Ercole II. and Renée of France. D'Estissac was the bearer of letters of commendation from Henry III. and the Queen Mother to the Duke of Ferrara.

him standing by a table awaiting us. He
raised his hand to his cap when we entered
and remained uncovered during the whole
of the conversation, which was somewhat
lengthy.   First of all he asked of M. de
Montaigne whether he could speak the language of the country, and, being answered
affirmatively, he said in most eloquent wise,
speaking Italian, that it pleased him greatly
to see gentlemen of our nation, he himself
being the very obedient servant of his most
Christian Majesty.   They conversed together
on several other matters, and then we retired,
the duke having kept himself uncovered all
through the interview.

In one of the churches we saw an effigy
of Ariosto,[1] the face being somewhat fuller
than in the one given in his works. He
died at the age of fifty-nine on June 6, 1533.
Here they served us fruit on plates.   The
streets are all paved with bricks, but the
arcades, which are everywhere to be found

[1] In the church of S. Benedetto.   It is now removed
to the library.

in Padua, and are vastly convenient for
walking at all times under cover and free
from mire, are wanting. In Venice the
streets are paved in similar fashion and on
the slope, so there is never any mud. I
forgot to remark that the day we quitted
Venice we met a number of boats filled with
fresh water, the contents of a boat being
worth a crown in Venice, where it is used
for drinking or dyeing cloth. After we got
to Fusina we saw how the water was raised
from a stream and turned into a canal by
means of a wheel kept going without ceasing
by horses. The boats aforesaid lie beneath
the mouth of the canal and are there loaded
with water.

We spent all this day at Ferrara and
visited there many fine churches, gardens,
and private houses, and all that was by
report worth seeing; amongst other things,
a rose bush at the monastery of the Jesuates
which flowers all the year round, and even
now they found thereon a rose which they
gave to M. de Montaigne. We saw likewise

the *Bucentaur*, which the duke, in emulation
of the one at Venice, had caused to be built
for his new wife,[1] who is fair and far too
young for him, in order that she may sail
in the same on the river Po.   Next we
visited the duke's arsenal, where there is a
piece of ordnance thirty-five spans in length
and having a bore one foot in diameter.
The thick new wine which we drank and
the turbid water drawn from the river made
M. de Montaigne fear an attack of colic.
On the door of every room in the inn is
an inscription, " *Ricordati della boletta*," and
immediately a stranger arrives he must
needs send his name and the number of his
attendants to the magistrate, who will then
give orders for lodgment, but if this be not
done no one will take them in.   On the
Thursday morning we set forth[2] over a

[1] Margherita Gonzaga, whom Alfonso married in 1579.
She was the daughter of Guglielmo, Duke of Mantua.
[2] It is strange that Montaigne should have made no
allusion in his journal to a visit which he paid to Tasso,
who had been imprisoned the year before in the hospital
of S. Anna at Ferrara.   In *Essais* ii. 12 he writes :
" Platon dit les mélancholiques plus disciplinables et

level, very fertile country, and one hard to
be traversed by foot passengers should the
ways be miry, because the soil of Lombardy
is very sticky. Moreover, the roads being
banked on either side, there is not space
enough to allow foot travellers to escape the
mud by walking on the unbroken ground,
wherefore many of the country folk go shod
with shoes half a foot high. We arrived at
Boulougne[1] in the evening, after travelling
thirty miles without a halt.

excellens ; aussi n'en est-il point qui ayent tant de pro-
pension à la folie. Infinis esprits se treuvent ruinez par
leur propre force et souplesse. Quel saut vient de
prendre de sa propre agitation et allegresse, l'un des
plus judicieux, ingenieux, et plus formez à l'air de cette
antique et pure Poësie, qu'autre Poëte Italien aye jamais
este ? N'a-il pas de quoy sçavoir gré à cette sienne
vivacité meurtrière ? à cette clarté qui l'a aveuglé ? à cette
exacte et tenduë apprehension de la raison, qu'il a mis
sans raison ? à la curieuse et laborieuse queste des
Sciences, qui l'a conduict à la bestise ? à cette rare
aptitude aux exercises de l'ame qui l'a rendu sans
exercise et sans ame ? J'eus plus de dépit encore que de
compassion de le voir à Ferrare en si pitieux estat,
survivant à soy mesme, mescognoisant et soy et ses
ouvrages ; les quels sans son sçeu et toutefois à sa veuë,
on a mis en lumière incorrigez et informe."

[1] Bologna.   :

This is a fine handsome town, larger and
much more populous than Ferrara. At the same
house in which we lodged the young Seigneur
de Montluc had arrived an hour sooner than
ourselves, having come from France to this
city to learn riding and the use of arms.
On the Friday we witnessed some sword
play by a certain Venetian, who boasted of
having discovered some new tricks in the
art of fencing, all the others following his
lead; in sooth his style differs vastly from
the ordinary sword exercise. The best of
his pupils was a young Bordelais named
Binet. We saw there a square clock tower,
very ancient, which leaned over so much
that it threatened to fall in ruins; also the
School of Sciences, which is the finest building
devoted to such uses I ever beheld. On the
Saturday after dinner we saw a play by the
comedians, with which M. de Montaigne
was highly pleased, but from this, or some
other cause, he was troubled afterwards with
headache, a distemper which had not molested
him for several years, but it passed away

EXEMPLAR·FONTIS·EXIMIAE
BONONIENSI·PVBLICAE
FACTAE·IN·VRBE·MEDIA·

PVLCHRITVDINIS·S·P·Q·
VTILIATIS·ET·ORNATVS·GRATIA·
ANNO·MD·LXIII·

FOUNTAIN AT BOLOGNA

To face p. 38, vol. ii.

during the night. Moreover at this time he professed to be freer of pain in the kidneys than for a long while, and rejoiced in digestive powers as sane as when he returned from Banieres.

This city is everywhere adorned with fine rich porticoes and a multitude of beautiful palaces. The cost of living here was very cheap, about the same as at Padua, but the city is turbulent in some of the older parts, which are divided between the ancient families of the city, some of whom favour the French [1] and others the Spaniards, who abound. In the great square is a very beautiful fountain.[2] On Sunday M. de Montaigne had made up his mind to take the left-hand road towards Imola, the March of Ancona and Loreto, on the way to Rome,

[1] The Collegio di Spagna, the only separate college which still exists, was founded by Cardinal d'Albornoz in 1364. There was doubtless a French college for students at the time of Montaigne's visit.

[2] This fountain was built while Cardinal Borromeo was legate. It was designed by Lauretti, a Sicilian, the statues being the work of Gian Bologna.

but a certain German told him that he had been plundered by outlaws in the duchy of Spoleto,[1] so he followed the highway to the right to Florence. We found ourselves at once on a rough road and in a mountainous country. After a sixteen-mile journey we rested for the night at Loyan,[2] a small and disagreeable village. In this place are only two hostelries, and these are famous all through Italy for the ill-faith there kept with travellers; how the host regales them with fair promises of all sorts of good cheer before they alight, and afterwards, when the strangers are at his mercy, will laugh in their faces. Concerning this are some well-known proverbs. We left early next morning and travelled till evening over a road which, certes, was the only bad one we had yet met

[1] Spoleto and the Bolognese territories as well were greatly overrun with brigands at this period. Large bands of armed ruffians ranged the country, nominally fighting one another, but really robbing and murdering the helpless peasants. One band, that of Sassomolari, was estimated to number four or five hundred men. Brigandage was not put down till the pontificate of Sixtus V.

[2] Lojano.

with. The mountains too gave more trouble than in any other part of our journeying. We lay that night, after riding four-and-twenty miles, at Scarperia, a small village of Tuscany. Here they sell cases of needles and scissors and other similar wares. M. de Montaigne was there greatly diverted over the dispute of the innkeepers. These people are wont to despatch lackeys distances of seven or eight leagues to meet strangers, and to urge them to alight at their employer's inn. It is no rare thing to find the host himself on horseback, and often a troop of men finely clad will follow on your track. All along this road M. de Montaigne was fain to jest with them, being vastly amused at the various offers every one of them made to him, and there was nothing they would not promise. One went so far as to offer the gift of a hare if only he would patronise a particular inn. This wrangle and grabbing ceased whenever we reached the town gates, beyond which they dare not say a word on the subject.

A general practice with all innkeepers is to offer at their own charges a guide on horseback to show the way, and to carry some portion of the baggage to the lodging taken. I know not whether they are obliged by law to do this on account of the insecurity of the highways. At Lojano, and in travelling from Boulougne, we always made a bargain as to price paid and accommodation received, and now, on account of the urgency of the innkeepers and others, M. de Montaigne sent forward always some one or other of the company to inspect the rooms, the provisions, and the wines, and to gather knowledge as to how he would fare, before he should get off his horse. Then he would go to the house of which he got the best report. But the most careful specification will not guard entirely against the knavery of these people, for they will keep you short either of wood, or candles, or linen, or of horse provender, which you may have forgotten to mention. Many travellers pass along this route, as it is the high road to

Rome. I was informed of a foolish omission on my part, to wit, that I had neglected to visit, ten miles on this side of Lojano and two miles off the road, the summit of a mountain from which, in times of rain and storm or in the night, lofty flames may be seen to issue.[1] My informant told me that at certain times it sent forth with a mighty shock small pieces of metal of the shape of coins. This is a sight which ought not to have been missed.

On the morning of the morrow we left Scarperia with our host as guide, traversing a fine road through poplars and well-tilled slopes. At the second mile we turned off the road to the right to see the palace which the Duke of Florence has been building for the last two years, using all the five senses in its embellishment. It seems as if he had advisedly chosen an inconvenient, sterile, and monotonous site—for instance, there is no

---

[1] I fuochi di Pietramala. There are emanations of coal gas from the rocks. At Acqua Buja, about a mile distant, the gas rises through the water of a small lake and ignites if fire be applied to it.

water—in order that he might have the honour of fetching the same five miles' distance, and his sand and lime another five. The site is nowhere level, and gives a view of several of those small hills which are everywhere a feature in this region. The palace itself is called Pratellino.[1] Seen from afar, the building has a mean aspect, but a close inspection shows it very fair, but not equal to the finest of our French mansions. They say it contains a hundred-and-twenty furnished chambers, and ten or twelve of the finest of these we saw, the furniture being pretty but not magnificent. There are several curiosities, a grotto constructed with divers niches and apartments which

[1] Pratolino, a villa built in 1573 by Francesco dei Medici, Grand Duke of Florence. Little now remains of it save some out-buildings, the colossal statue of L'Appennino, and some of the waterworks in which Montaigne found so much to admire. It was built from the design of Bernardo Buontalenti, but some portions— not the statue aforesaid—were the work of Gian Bologna. The villa seems to have been in existence at the beginning of the present century. The park now belongs to Prince Demidoff.

exceeds anything of the kind we have seen
elsewhere. It is encrusted and modelled all
through with a certain material brought from
the mountains, the joints being fastened together with invisible nails. Not only is
music and harmony made to sound by water
power; statues move and doors open,
animals dive and drink, and other similar
results are caused by the same force. By a
single movement the whole grotto can be
filled with water, and all the seats will squirt
water over your breech; then, as you flee
from the grotto and run up the staircase
into the mansion on the other side, a pleasant
trick will make the water stream from two
of the steps in a thousand jets which drench
you till you reach the top. The beauty and
splendour of this place cannot be set forth
properly by details. Below the mansion is an
alley, fifty feet wide and about five hundred
paces in length, which at great cost has been
made almost level.[1] On either side are long
and very beautiful benches of worked stone,

[1] This alley is still in existence.

every five or every ten paces. Along by these benches are built in the wall the mouths of artificial fountains, so that all down the alley are jets of water. At the end is a fair fountain discharging itself into a great basin through a marble statue, carved in the similitude of a woman starching linen. She is represented wringing a tablecloth, fashioned in marble, and it is in dripping from this cloth that the water finds its way out. Below is another vessel to contain the hot water for making the starch.

In a chamber of the mansion is a marble table with places for six, each of which is fitted with a cover to be raised by a ring. Beneath each of these covers is a basin with a supply of fresh water, wherewith each guest might cool his glass, and in the middle of the table a large space for the bottle. We saw also great holes in the ground where a large quantity of snow was kept all through the year., It is set upon litter of broom and then covered with straw in high pyramidal form like a small barn.

There are a thousand reservoirs; and the duke was at this time busied in making a colossus, the eye-socket of which is three cubits in width and all the rest in proportion.[1] The thousand reservoirs and pools are supplied from two springs through a vast number of earthen pipes. In a large and beautiful bird-cage we saw some little birds resembling goldfinches, with two long tail feathers like large capons; and there is also a curious hothouse. We tarried some two or three hours in this place, and then, having resumed our journey, we went for seventeen miles along the crest of divers small hills and arrived at Florence.

This is a smaller town than Ferrara, placed in a plain and surrounded by a vast number of well-cultivated hills. The Arno, which is crossed by divers bridges, runs through it and the walls of the town have no ditches. This day M. de Montaigne passed two stones and a large amount of

[1] L'Appennino, erroneously attributed to Gian Bologna. It was repaired in 1877 by Prince Demidoff.

gravel without perceiving anything more than a slight pain in the lower part of the stomach. On the same day we visited the stables[1] of the Grand Duke, which are large and arched in the roofs, but no valuable horses were therein. The Grand Duke is not at present in residence. We saw there a strange kind of sheep, a camel, some lions and bears, and an animal as big as a large mastiff, the shape of a cat, and spotted black and white, which they called a tiger. We went to the church of Saint Lawrence where those banners of ours which Marshal Strozzi[2] lost in his Tuscan defeat are still hanging. In this same church are several specimens of painting on the flat, and some beautiful statues of excellent workmanship,

[1] These were in the Piazza S. Marco. They were built by Lorenzo, Duke of Urbino, in 1515. In 1550 Cosimo transferred to an adjoining site the wild animals which had been hitherto kept in the Palazzo Vecchio. The Grand Duke alluded to was Francesco, son of Cosimo I.

[2] This was the Strozzi whose tomb Montaigne had recently visited at Epernay (vol. i. p. 31). He was defeated by the Spaniards and Imperialists at Lucignano in 1554.

the work of Michael Angelo.[1] We next
saw the Dome, a very large church, and the
bell tower, covered with black and white
marble and one of the fairest and richest
works in the world. M. de Montaigne
affirmed that he never saw a nation so lacking in fair women as the Italian,[2] and the
lodgment he found far less well arranged
than in France or Germany; the food,
indeed, was not half so abundant or well
served as in Germany. In neither country
is the meat larded, but in Germany it is
far better seasoned, and there is greater
variety in sauces and soups. The rooms
themselves in Italy are vastly inferior, no
saloons, the windows large, and all uncovered save by a huge wooden shutter,

---

[1] The statues in the Medici Chapel.

[2] In *Essais*, iii. 5, he writes in a more charitable strain :
"Ceux qui connoissent l'Italie, ne trouveront jamais
estrange, si pour ce sujet je ne cherche ailleurs des
examples. Car cette nation se peut dire regente du
reste du Monde en cela. Ils ont plus communément
de belles femmes, et moins de laides que nous : mais
des rares et excellentes beautez, j'estime que nous allons
à pair."

which would exclude all daylight if it should be necessary to keep off the sun or the wind, an inconvenience which M. de Montaigne found still more intolerable than the lack of curtains in Germany. The chambers are wretched boxes, meanly curtained, and never more than one set in a room. Under the hangings is a bed on castors, and any one who is averse to lying hard will find himself in evil case. There is as great, or greater, want of linen; and the wines are for the most part inferior, and at this season undrinkable by all who dislike a mawkish sweetness. The price of everything is indeed somewhat lower; Florence, however, is reputed to be one of the dearest towns in Italy. Before my master arrived I made a bargain at the hostelry of the "Angel"[1] for seven reals a day for man and horse, and four reals for the servants.

On this same day we inspected one of the

[1] "L'hostelerie de l'Ange," probably now "L'albergo dell' Agnolo" in the Borgo S. Lorenzo.

duke's palaces, where certain men were engaged in counterfeiting eastern jewels, and working in crystal ; for this prince is somewhat given to alchemy and the mechanic arts, and is above all a great architect. On the morrow M. de Montaigne went first to the top of the Dome, where he saw the ball of gilded bronze, which from below seems about the bigness of a bullet, but which, when one is thereby, proves capable of holding forty men. He inspected the marble, variegated and carved throughout, with which this church is encrusted, and found that even the black sort was already showing signs of decay in many places through the action of the frost and snow, wherefore he began to doubt whether it was really genuine. He was minded likewise to visit the palaces of the Strozzi and the Gondi,[1] which were still occupied by certain members of the said families, as well as the duke's palace where Cosimo, the father of the reigning duke,

[1] Members of both these families had migrated to France.

had caused to be painted the capture of
Siena and scenes in the battle we lost.[1] In
divers places in the city, and notably in the
palace aforesaid and on the ancient walls, the
fleur de lys holds the first place of honour.
M. d'Estissac and M. de Montaigne went
to dine with the Grand Duke. His wife[2] was
seated in the place of honour, and the duke
below her, then the sister-in-law of the
duchess, and then her brother the husband
of the aforesaid. According to the Italian
taste the duchess is handsome, with an agree-
able and inspiring face, full bust, and a bosom
displaying itself as it may. M. de Montaigne fully recognised in her the charm by
which she has been able to cajole this prince
and to insure his devotion for a long time.
The duke is a big dark man of about my

[1] The battle of Marciano. The great hall in the
Palazzo Vecchio was painted by Vasari to celebrate the
triumphs of Cosimo I.

[2] The notorious Bianca Capello. The Grand Duke
had married her the preceding year. The almost simul-
taneous death of these two at Poggio a Cajano in 1587 is
one of the mysterious crimes of history.

own height,[1] large-limbed, with a face beam-
ing with courtesy, and always wont to go
uncovered through the crowd of servants,
which thing is very seemly. His appearance
is that of a healthy man of forty. On the
other side of the table sat the cardinal[2] and
another young man of eighteen, brothers of
the duke. The attendants brought to the
duke and the duchess a basin in which were
placed a glass full of wine, uncovered, and a
glass bottle full of water. Having taken the
glass of wine, they poured into the basin
as much thereof as they willed, and refilled
the glass with water. Then they replaced
the glass in the basin which the attendant
held before them. The duke put into his

---

[1] *De ma taille.* Although the secretary is writing the
comparison is evidently with Montaigne himself.

[2] Ferdinando, son of Cosimo I. He renounced his
orders and succeeded his brother in 1587. He also was
at Poggio when the tragedy happened, and it was commonly believed that Bianca intended to poison him, but
Duke Francesco inadvertently drank the poisoned wine.
The younger brother was probably Giovanni, a son of
Cosimo I. by Eleanora d'Albizzi, born in 1562. The tragic
fate of this prince and of his brother Garcia is one of the
mysteries of Italian family crime.

wine due quantity of water, the duchess scarcely any. The bad habit of the Germans in using glasses of an inordinate size is here reversed, seeing that in Italy the wine glasses are exceedingly small.

I cannot tell why this city should be termed " beautiful," as it were by privilege. Beautiful it is, but no more so than Bologna, and little more than Ferrara, while it falls far short of Venice. You may indeed discern from the top of the bell tower innumerable houses, which cover the hills all around for the distance of two or three leagues ; and in the plain, some two leagues in extent, on which the city stands, they seem to touch, so closely are they built one to another. The city is paved with flat stones without pattern or regularity. After the dinner the four gentlemen and a guide took the post to go to visit a place belonging to the duke which is called *Castello*.[1] There is nothing of merit in the house, but around it are divers gardens, the entire place being set on the slope

[1] Petraja.

of a hill, so that the main walks are on the slope, and the cross alleys straight and level; also many arbours, thickly covered with interwoven twigs of sweet-smelling shrubs, such as cedar, cypress, orange, citron, and olive, the branches being enlaced so closely that the sun at his fiercest could not pierce thereinside. The undergrowth of these cypresses and other trees is so close that only three or four persons can pass together through it.   Amongst the ponds there is a large one, in the midst of which stands a rock, imitated from nature, which, by the application of the same material used by the duke in covering his grottoes at Pratellino, looks as if it were glazed over; and above it is a large casting of copper worked into the likeness of a hoary old man seated on his breech with crossed arms.   From his beard, his forehead, and his skin, there is a perpetual drip of water representing tears and sweat, and indeed this drip is the sole supply of the basin.

In another part of the garden they encountered a very humorous experience, for,

as they were walking about therein and
marking its curiosities, the gardener for a
certain purpose withdrew, and while they
stood gazing at some marble statues, there
sprang up under their feet and between their
legs an infinite number of tiny jets of water,
so minute that they resembled exactly
drops of rain, and with this they were
sprinkled all over. It was produced by the
working of subterranean machinery which
the gardener, being two hundred paces distant, set in motion. So delicately was it
constructed that he was able from where he
was stationed to raise and depress the outflow
as he willed. The same device is to be found
in divers other places. They saw also the
great fountain which finds a channel through
two vast bronze figures, one of which, clasped
by the other in a violent embrace, seems half-
fainting, and, with head thrown back, belches
forth the stream from his mouth. So great is
the force that the column of water rises some
thirty-seven fathoms above the top of these
figures, which are themselves twenty feet

high. Here is a little chamber made amongst the boughs of an evergreen tree of a much more luxuriant growth than any other they had yet seen. It is entirely clipped out of the green boughs of the tree aforesaid, so that there is no prospect to be got therefrom, save through certain apertures which it has been necessary to make here and there, by clearing away the branches. In the midst of the chamber, from pipes which are concealed, rises a fountain which is set in the middle of a marble table. By a certain device the water made music, but this they were not able to hear, for it would have been too late for people who had to return to the city. They saw likewise the coat-of-arms of the duke over a gateway, excellently formed from the branches of trees fostered and restrained in their natural growth by certain ligaments which could scarcely be discerned. Their visit was paid in the season when gardens have their worst aspect, wherefore the wonder was all the greater. Besides the things described above they saw a beautiful grotto, in

which were fashioned all sorts of animals
after nature, every one of which gave out
the water of the fountains, either from the
beak or the wing, or the talon, or the ear, or
the nostril. I forgot to say that in the palace
of this prince there is the figure of a quadru-
ped in bronze after nature, of a very strange
form, which is set up on a column.[1] The
foreparts are scaly, and upon the back are
members of a fashion I cannot describe—
somewhat like horns. The story is that it
was discovered in a 'cave in the adjacent
mountains and brought hither alive several
years ago. We saw likewise the palace of
the Queen Mother[2]; and M. de Montaigne,
according to his wont, was minded to test the
capabilities of the city by looking at rooms
which were to let and boarding-houses, but
he found none worth notice. From what was
told him it appeared that lodgings were only
to be had at the hostelries, and the private

[1] The image of the Chimera, now in the Etruscan
Museum. It was dug up at Arezzo in 1559.
[2] Catherine dei Medici.

apartments which he saw were far more costly
than those of Paris, or even of Venice.   The
table was mean, and cost more than twelve
crowns per mensem for the gentlefolk. In this
city no seemly diversion was to be had, neither
in arms, nor horsemanship, nor letters.[1]   Pewter ware is very scarce in these parts, the
service being made on vessels of painted
earthenware none too clean.

[1] This is probably one of those traveller's hasty
generalisations which Montaigne occasionally lets drop.
In his second visit he modified several of his earlier
statements, and a very slight inquiry would have served
to show him that letters still flourished in Florence,
though not so freely as in the golden time of the earlier
Medici.   The *Accademia Fiorentina* was founded in
1540, and the year following his visit saw the beginning
of the Della Crusca.

VI

JOURNEY TO ROME

ON the morning of Thursday, November 24, we departed and found ourselves in a country fairly fertile, thickly peopled, and everywhere under tillage. The road was uneven and stony, and, after a very long journey, we arrived late at night at Siena, thirty-two miles, or four posts, which here they reckon of eight miles, somewhat longer than ours usually are. On the Friday we examined the place carefully, especially with respect to our own military operations there-in.[1] The site of the city is very irregular, for it is built on the ridge of a hill, where

---

[1] During the mediæval wars Siena always favoured the French party. Villani (i. 43, 56) gives the legendary French origin of the place: how in the eighth century Charles Martel marched against the Lombards in Apulia, and left those of his troops who were old and unfit for

most of the streets are to be found.   Other
thoroughfares lead down the slopes on either
side by means of steps, some of these mount-
ing the opposite hill to various levels.   The
city is about the same size as Florence, and
one of the fairest of Italy, but not of the first
order, its great antiquity being proclaimed
by its aspect.   Everywhere fountains are
plentiful, but it is said that individual persons
draw water privately from the conduits for
their particular use.   Here are to be found
fine cool cellars.   The Dome, which is scarcely
inferior to that at Florence, is covered almost
entirely within and without with marble of
the place : square pieces, some a foot thick,
some less, are used for panelling the same,
for they always cover thus buildings of brick,
the common building material of this land.
The most beautiful portion of the city is
the circular market-place, a fine expanse which

service at this place.   Two refuges were built, and the
name *Sena* given to them, on account of the old men who
dwelt therein.   Villani calls it, for this reason, one of
the most modern of Italian cities, ignoring Julius Cæsar's
foundation altogether.

slopes from all sides towards the palace, which
in itself forms one of the segments of the
circle, somewhat less curved than the rest.
In front of the palace, and at the highest
point of the market-place, is a very beautiful
fountain, which discharges itself by several
pipes, and fills a great basin where any one
may take at will the purest water.[1] Several
streets open into this place, the pavement
being set in steps.   In the town are many
streets, certain of them being very ancient.
The chief of these is the Piccolomini, then the
Tolomei, the Colombini and the Cerretani.[2]

---

[1] The Fonte Gaja, which was completed in 1343. The
sculptured reliefs were added by Jacopo della Quercia,
1412–1419.   The sculptor subsequently enjoyed the
epithet "della Fonte."   It was well restored by Signor
Sarocchi in recent times.   Dante's eulogy of the market-
place is well known :—

> "Quando vivea pui glorioso, disse
>   Liberamente nel Campo di Siena,
>   Ogni vergogna deposta, s'affise."
>
> *Purg.*, xi.

[2] These names all belong to the ancient Sienese
nobility, and it is almost certain that Montaigne is referring
to palaces and not to streets.

We saw indications of an antiquity of three or four hundred years. The arms of the city, which are displayed on columns in several places, represent the she-wolf which gave suck to Romulus and Remus.

The Duke of Florence treats with courtesy the nobles who are in our interest, and keeps about his person Silvio Piccolomini, a gentleman who is better endowed than any other of our day in all sorts of science and in the practice of arms.[1] The duke being chiefly concerned in guarding himself from his own subjects, leaves to his various cities the duty of fortifying themselves, but keeps a hold on the citadels, which are provisioned and guarded with great outlay of money and labour, and with such watchful suspicion that

[1] He was one of the most celebrated captains of the age. He fought in almost every country in Europe, and was equally distinguished as a man of affairs and a courtier, as he managed to retain to his death the favour and confidence of successive Grand Dukes of Tuscany. His son, Ottavio, was the well-known general of the Thirty Years' War. He died in 1614, and is buried in the church of S. Agostino at Siena.

few people are allowed to approach them.
The women mostly wear bonnets, and we
marked some who, by way of reverence,
removed their headgear like the men at the
moment of the elevation of the Host.   We
found lodging at the " Crown," [1] which was
fairly good, but we had no glass or even linen
windows.

M. de Montaigne, when he was asked by
the house-steward at Pratellino whether
he was not amazed at the beauty of the
place, replied, after certain words of praise,
that he was greatly offended by the ill-
seeming of the doors and windows, and of
the great pinewood tables, without shape or
ornament; with the rude and insecure locks,
like those used in our villages, and with the
roofs of hollow tiles.   Moreover, he declared
that, if it were found impossible to conceal
these tiles by the use of slate or lead or brass,
they might at least keep them out of sight
by the arrangement of the building, and the

---

[1] This house is probably No. 32 in what is now the
Via Cavour.   It was an hotel as late as 1852.

steward said he would carry this counsel to
his master.

The duke leaves unmolested the ancient
marks and devices of the city, which everywhere echo the cry of "Liberty." Again,
as to the tombs and epitaphs of the French
who died here, they have removed them to
a remote corner of the town, under the pre-
tence of some reconstruction and rebuilding
of the church wherein they were placed. On
Saturday the 26th, after dinner, we went
twelve miles through a country resembling
the last we traversed, and arrived in time for
supper at Buonconvento, a Tuscan *Castello*, a
word they apply to the walled villages which,
from their smallness, do not merit the name
of town. Early on Sunday morning we
departed therefrom, and because M. de Montaigne desired to see Montalcino, on account
of the associations of the French therewith, he
turned off the road to the right and, with
M. d'Estissac, M. de Mattecoulon, and M. du
Hautoy, repaired to the town aforesaid, which
they described as an ill-built place, about the

size of Saint Emilion,[1] situated on the top of the highest mountain of the district, but still accessible. They heard High Mass which was being said there. At one end of the town is a castle garrisoned for the duke, but M. de Montaigne was of opinion that it was faulty as a stronghold, being commanded on one side by another mountain some hundred paces distant.

In the duke's dominions the people hold the French in such great affection that the awakening of any memory of our country will almost certainly bring tears to their eyes. It would seem that they prefer even war, with some form of freedom, to the peace they enjoy under their tyrant. M. de Montaigne inquired whether there were not certain French tombs in the town,[2] and was

[1] A town near Bordeaux.
[2] After the capture of Siena by the Spaniards in 1555 a number of the people of Siena, nobles as well as burghers, withdrew to Montalcino with the intention of founding there a new republic. With them went the French mercenaries who, under the Marshal de Monluc, had helped to defend the city. Montaigne was, no doubt, inquiring after the tombs of these men.

informed that these formerly were in the
church of S. Agostino, but that by the command of the duke the remains had been buried
in the earth.   Our road lay through a
mountainous, stony country for twenty-three
miles, and in the evening we came to La
Paille, a little village of five or six houses,
at the foot of sterile and forbidding mountains.   Early next morning we resumed our
journey, traversing a deep and very stony
valley, and passing and repassing a hundred
times a torrent which flowed through the
same.   At the limit of the duke's territory
we came to a fine bridge, built by Pope
Gregory,[1] and entered the States of the
Church, coming first to Acquapendente, a
small town which, as I believe, takes its
name from a torrent hard by which falls
from the rocks down on to the plain.   Then
we passed a *Castello*, called S. Lorenzo, and
another, Bolsena, and turning round the Lake

---

[1] This bridge crosses a stream called La Paglia, to
which Montaigne probably refers when he speaks of the
village of La Paille.

of Bolsena, which is thirty miles long, ten
wide, and has in its midst islands on which
they say are monasteries, we went in one
bout of twenty-six miles over a rocky and
barren road to Montefiascone, a little town
placed on the summit of one of the highest
mountains in the country.   It is very small,
but shows signs of great antiquity.   We
quitted it next morning, and crossed a fine
fertile plain, in which is situated Viterbo,
part of the town being built on the crest of a
hill.   This is a fine place, about the size of
Senlis, in which we observed many handsome
houses, numerous workmen, fair pleasant
streets, and three very beautiful fountains
in divers parts of the town.   On account
of the beauty of the place M. de Montaigne
would fain have tarried there, but his baggage
mule, which he sent in advance, had already
passed onward.   Here we began the ascent
of the flank of a high mountain, and at the
end of the descent on the farther side we
came upon the little Lake of Vico.   Then,
having traversed a delightful valley, bordered

by gentle hills rich in wood—a commodity
very rare in these parts—and by the lake
aforesaid, we found ourselves in good time at
Rossiglione,[1] after riding nineteen miles.

This is a small town, with a castle belonging to the Duke of Parma; indeed, along
this road are to be found several mansions
and estates belonging to the Farnese family.
Lodging on this road is of the best, inasmuch as it is the great post road. They
charge five giulios[2] for the hire of a horse,
and two for the post, and they make the
same terms if the horses are hired for two
or three posts, or for several days, in which
case the hirer has no trouble about the
horses; for, from one place to another, the
innkeepers take charge of those belonging to
their neighbours, and, moreover, they will
make a contract under which you may be
supplied with a fresh horse elsewhere on the
road in case one of your own should fail.

[1] Ronciglione. The Farnesi had one of their finest
seats here.

[2] A piece of money first coined by Julius III., worth
about sixty centesimi.

At Siena we saw for ourselves how a man trusted a horse to a certain Fleming, who was travelling in company with us, alone, unknown, and a stranger to the owner of the horse, simply on the condition that the horse hire should be paid before starting. In every other respect the horse is at your disposal, under your promise that you will leave him where you have agreed. M. de Montaigne, adapting himself, as was his wont, to the custom of the country, fell into the way of dining early and supping late, for in the good houses the dinner is only served at noon, and the supper at nine o'clock; for instance, in these places where we found playhouses the acting began by torchlight at six, and lasted two or three hours; then we returned to sup. M. de Montaigne would remark that this was a good country for lazy folk, seeing the hour of rising was so late.

On the morrow we set forth three hours before daybreak, so keenly was M. de Montaigne set on seeing the Roman plain by day. He found the cold air of morning as hurtful to his stomach as that of the evening,[1] and was ill at ease till sunrise, though the night was fine. After the fifteenth milestone we caught sight of the city of Rome: then we lost it for some long time. On the road we passed several villages and inns. We came upon some portions of road, elevated and paved with large stones, having about them a certain look of antiquity; and nearer to the city we remarked some masonry, evidently of great age, and stones which the Popes had caused to be reinstated on account of their antiquarian interest. The greater part of the ruins—the baths of Diocletian, for instance—are of bricks, small and plain like those we use, and not of the size and thickness of those we see in the ancient ruins of France and elsewhere. On our road the city did not show itself very plainly. Far on the left

[1] Montaigne evidently feared the effect of the dew. Just before he reached Roveredo (vol. i. p. 187) he writes to the same effect.

hand were the Apennines, the aspect of the country being unpleasing, rugged, full of deep clefts, and unfitted for the passage of troops or ordnance. All the land is treeless, and a good part of it sterile, and lying open for ten miles and more, the houses being very sparse, as in all countries of this sort. Travelling thus we went thirty miles, and arrived on the last day of November—Saint Andrew's day—at the Porta del Popolo of Rome.

VII

ROME

HERE they raised difficulties as in other places concerning the plague raging at Genoa. We went to lodge at the "Bear,"[1] and stayed there the following day also, and on the 2nd of December we hired apartments in the house of a Spaniard in front of Santa Lucia della Tinta.[2] We were well accommodated in three fine chambers, a living room, a larder, a stable, and a kitchen, for twenty crowns a month, the host finding in addition a cook and fire in the kitchen. Here the apartments are as a rule furnished somewhat better than in Paris, inasmuch as they use much gilded leather in the upholstering of

[1] This inn still exists at the corner of the Via di Monte Brianza and the Via dell' Orso.
[2] In the Via di Monte Brianza.

all houses of consideration.   We might have had lodging at the " Vaso d'Oro " hard by at the same price, furnished with silk and cloth of gold such as kings use, but M. de Montaigne objected, first because the chambers had no separate entrances, and next because the magnificence of this furniture was not only useless in itself, but liable to give great trouble in keeping it from hurt, each bed being of the value of four or five hundred crowns.   At our lodging we made a bargain for a supply of linen, as we should have done in France, but of this, as is the way of the country, they were somewhat sparing.

M. de Montaigne was annoyed to find such great number of Frenchmen in Rome,[1] so great that almost every person he met in the streets addressed him in his own tongue.   He found novelty in the sight of so mighty a court, thronged with prelates and churchmen, and declared that Rome was far fuller of rich men and coaches and

[1] He makes the same complaint of Padua.

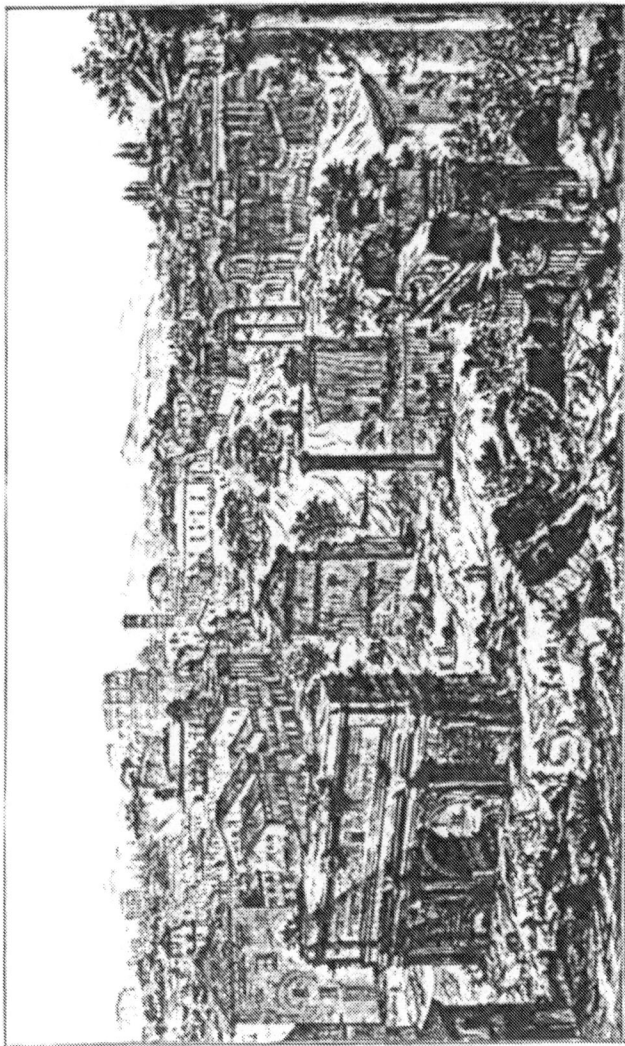

THE ROMAN FORUM FROM THE CAPITOL.

From Piranesi's Views of Rome

horses than any other city he had ever seen, and that the seeming of the streets in various ways, and notably in the crowds of people, reminded him more of Paris than of any other place. The present city is placed along either bank of the Tiber. The hilly quarter, where the ancient city stood, and whither M. de Montaigne went every day to walk and to survey the site, is now divided between certain churches, and rich houses and gardens belonging to the cardinals. He found clear evidence to show that the configuration and slopes of the hills had altogether changed since ancient times. He judged from the height of the ruins, and was fully assured that in certain places we were walking over the roof-ridges of houses still intact; indeed it is easy to see by the state of the Arch of Severus that we now stand more than two pikes' length above the ancient level, and that we walk on the tops of the old walls, which the rains and the coach wheels occasionally bring into sight.

M. de Montaigne would not admit that
liberty existed in Rome equal to that enjoyed in Venice, and would advance by way
of arguments the facts that houses were so insecure against robbers that people who might
bring home with them a large amount of
property usually determined to give their
purses in charge of the bankers of the city
so as not to find their strong boxes rifled,
which mishap had befallen many; that it
was by no means safe to walk abroad by
night; that in this month of December the
General of the Cordeliers had been suddenly
deprived of his office and imprisoned because in his preaching, at which were present the Pope and the cardinals, he had
censured the sloth and luxury of the prelates
of the Church, and this without mentioning
names and simply using commonplace remarks on the subject with a certain harsh-
ness of voice; that his own boxes had been
searched by the tax-officers on entering the
city and turned over even to the smallest
articles of apparel, while in the other towns

of Italy the officers had been satisfied by the
presentation of the boxes for search; that
in addition they had seized all the books
they found there with the view of inspecting
them, over which task they spent so much
time that any one in different case might
well have given up the books as lost. Again
the regulations were so extraordinary that
one of these books, the "Hours of our
Lady," having been printed at Paris and
not in Rome, was looked at with suspicion,
as were certain books against heretics by
German doctors who, in argument, happened
to make mention of the errors of their oppo-
nents. At this juncture he congratulated
himself over his good fortune in that, having
no premonition of the search which awaited
him, and having passed through Germany
where forbidden books abound, he had not
brought away with him a single one of
these, notwithstanding the curious interest
which often possessed him with regard to
divers of them. Certain gentlemen from
Germany informed him that had any such

volume been found, he would have paid the penalty by losing all his books.

On Christmas Day we went to hear the Papal Mass at St. Peter's, M. de Montaigne being accommodated with a seat from which he could behold at his ease all the ceremonial. . They used certain particular forms; to wit, they read the Gospel and the Epistle first in Latin and then in Greek, a custom followed also on Easter Day, and on the feast of St. Peter. The Pope himself[1] let divers others communicate, and with him officiated the Cardinals Farnese,[2] Medici,[3] Caraffa,[4] and Gonzaga. In taking the cup they use a certain instrument to

[1] Gregory XIII. Ugo Buoncompagni di Bologna.

[2] Alessandro Farnese, nephew of Paul III.

[3] Ferdinando dei Medici, the cardinal whom Montaigne had recently met at the Grand Duke's table in Florence.

[4] This Caraffa was first advanced by his kinsman, Paul IV., but banished on the accession of Pius IV. Pius V. restored him to his offices, and Gregory XIII. made him librarian of the Vatican. In *Essais*, i. 51, Montaigne writes "d'un Italien, que je vien d'entretenir, qui a servy le feu Cardinal Caraffe de maistre d'hotel jusques à sa mort."

prevent danger of poison.[1] It seemed
strange to M. de Montaigne that, at this
mass and at others beside, the Pope and
cardinals and other prelates kept seated
with heads covered and talked together the
while. The whole ceremony indeed was
marked by splendour rather than by devotion. Touching the beauty of the Roman
ladies, M. de Montaigne affirmed that this
was not notable enough to raise the reputation of this city beyond all others; moreover that, as in Paris, the most remarkable
beauty belonged to those who made a market
of the same.

On December 29th M. d'Abein,[2] our ambassador, a learned gentleman and a long-

---

[1] The fistula, or pipe, through which the Pope drinks
the consecrated wine. It would hardly give, as Montaigne suggests, any security against poison; this would
be compassed by "pregustation" on the part of the sac-
ristan and the butler.

[2] Louis Chasteignier de la Roche Posay, seigneur
d'Abain. He went with Henry III. into Poland, and
was subsequently sent by Henry as ambassador to
Rome. He was afterwards charged by the Pope to
carry the papal absolution to Henry IV.

standing friend of M. de Montaigne, advised
him to go and kiss the feet of the Pope. M.
de Montaigne and M. d'Estissac went in the
coach of the ambassador, who, after he had
been granted an audience, caused them to be
called by the Pope's chamberlain. According
to custom, only the ambassador was with the
Pope, who had by his side a bell which he
would ring when he might wish any one to
be introduced. The ambassador was seated,
uncovered, at his left hand; the Pope himself never uncovers before any one, nor
can any ambassador remain covered in his
presence. M. d'Estissac entered first, then
M. de Montaigne, then M. de Mattecoulon,
and last M. d'Hautoy. After taking a step
or two into the chamber, in a corner of which
sits the Pope, the incomer, whoever he may
be, kneels and waits for the Pope to give him
benediction. This done, he will rise and
advance to the middle of the room, but a
stranger rarely approaches the Pope by going
direct across the floor, the more ordinary
practice being to turn to the left on enter-

ing, and then, after making a détour along the wall, to approach his chair. But when the stranger has gone half the distance he must kneel again on one knee, and, having received a second benediction, next advances as far as the thick carpet spread out some seven or eight feet in front of the Pope. Here he must kneel on both knees, while the ambassador who presents him kneels on one, and moves back the Pope's robe from his right foot, which is shod in a red shoe with a white cross thereupon. The kneeling stranger must keep himself in the same posture until he is close to the Pope's foot, and then bend down to kiss it. M. de Montaigne declared that the Pope raised the point of his foot a little. They all kissed it one after the other, making room for each other after the ceremony was done. Then the ambassador covered the Pope's foot, and, having risen to his seat, said what seemed necessary on behalf of M. d'Estissac and M. de Montaigne. The Pope, with courteous expression of face, admonished M. d'Estissac to cultivate learning and virtue, and M. de Montaigne to maintain the devotion he had always exhibited towards the Church and the interests of the most Christian King: whatever service he could do them they might depend on, this being an Italian figure of speech. They said nothing, but, having been blessed again before rising as a sign of dismissal, they went back in the same order. Each one retreats as it seems best, but the ordinary custom is to go backward, or at least sideways, so as always to look the Pope in the face. As in entering, each one kneels half-way on one knee for another benediction, and again at the door for the last.

The Pope in speaking Italian betrays his Bolognese descent, the idiom of this city being the worst in Italy; and besides this, his speech is halting by nature. In other respects he is a very fine old man, of medium height, and upright, with a face full of majesty, and a long white beard. His age is over eighty, and for his years he is the most healthy and vigorous man possible, troubled

neither with gout nor colic nor stomach com-
plaints nor oppression of any kind. By nature
he is kind, caring little about affairs of state,
a great builder, and in the last-named capa-
city he will leave a memory highly honoured
in Rome and elsewhere.   In almsgiving he
is somewhat excessive. Amongst other proofs
of this, [it may be recorded that he is wont to
help any girl of the lower orders in furnishing
her home on her marriage, and report says
that he shows the same liberality in ready
money.] [1]   Besides this, he has built colleges
for the Greeks, the English, the Scots, the
French, the Germans, and the Poles, endow-
ing each one with a perpetual revenue of ten
thousand crowns, over and beyond the vast
cost of building.   This he has done to bring
back to the Church the sons of the nations
aforesaid, who were corrupted by evil opinions
hostile to her.   There the pupils are lodged,
fed, clothed, and taught, and provided with
everything without the expense of a single

[1] The text from which the passage within brackets is
translated was written by Montaigne himself on the
margin of the MS.—*Querlon's note.*

quattrino of their own on any account. Vexatious public duties he readily lets fall on the backs of others, and shrinks from troubling himself therewith. He gives as many audiences as are demanded. His replies are brief and decisive, and it is loss of time to oppose them by fresh reasoning. Nothing will move him from a decision which he believes to be a just one; and even for his own son,[1] whom he loves passionately, he will not stir a finger against his idea of justice.[2] He gives advancement to his relatives, but without trenching

[1] Giacomo Buoncompagni, the illegitimate son of the Pope. His mother was a servant in the house of Girolamo, the Pope's brother, in Bologna, where Giacomo was born in 1548. He was brought up by his father, and his mother was afterwards dowered by Girolamo and married to a Milanese mason. After his education was finished he was appointed to numerous offices, his father having been made Pope in 1572, and the lordships of Vignola, Sora, Arce, Arpino, and Aquino were purchased for him. He was a soldier and a patron of letters, and a favourable example of his kind. He died in 1612.

[2] Montaigne is probably referring to the Pope's banishment of Giacomo to Perugia in 1576, on account of an attempt made by his son to protect a servant from the due operation of the law. With regard to nepotism Gregory was moderate. He made two of his nephews cardinals, but the well-known story tells how he ordered

upon the rights of the Church, which he
preserves intact. He has done magnificent
work in public buildings and in remodelling
the streets of the city. In sooth, it may
be said that his life and doings call for no
special remark, neither in one nor in the
other respect, but that his leaning is strongly
towards good.

On the last day of December these two[1]
dined with M. le Cardinal de Sens, who is
more strict in his observance of Roman ceremonies than any other Frenchman. The
Benedicite and the graces were very long, and
were said by two chaplains, who responded
one to the other as if they were saying the
office in church, and during the repast a
paraphrase in Italian of the gospel of the
day was read. Both before and after dinner
they all washed their hands, and to each one
a napkin was served for use at table. Before

his brother back to Bologna when he heard he was on
his way to Rome to ask for preferment. Ranke, i. 290.

[1] Probably Montaigne and the ambassador. The
Cardinal de Sens was Nicolas de Pelvi, afterwards
Archbishop of Reims.

the guests who sat beside or facing the host
—as a mark of special honour—they placed
the large silver trays with salt cellars, made
like those which are put before guests of
worship in France.   Upon these trays was a
napkin folded in four, and on the napkin
was laid bread, a knife, a fork, and a spoon,
and over all another napkin for use at table,
the one first-named being left undisturbed.
After the guests had seated themselves
another plate of silver or earthenware would
be placed beside the silver tray aforesaid, and
this the guest would use during the repast.
The carver gives a portion of whatever is
served at table to all those seated, who never
touch the dishes with their hands.   Moreover, the dish set before the host is rarely
shared by any of the guests.

   To M. de Montaigne they served drink
as they usually served it at the ambassador's
house whenever he dined there; that is, they
brought him a silver basin in which was a
glass with wine, and a little bottle about the
size of those used for ink full of water.   He

took the glass in his right hand, and in his left the bottle, from which he poured as much water as he desired into the glass, and then replaced the bottle in the basin. When he drank the servant who waited on him held the basin below his chin, and afterwards replaced the glass in the basin aforesaid, such ceremony being observed only in the case of one or two sitting near the host. After the grace the table broke up at once, and the chairs were arranged along one side of the hall, where M. le Cardinal made them sit after he had seated himself. Two church-men, finely clad, and bearing in their hands certain instruments of a kind I had never seen before, now appeared; and, having knelt down, they recited a church service of some kind or other. The cardinal said nothing to them, but as they rose to depart, after having finished their service, he slightly moved his cap. A short time afterwards he took his guests in his coach to the Consistory Hall, where the cardinals were assembled for vespers. The Pope came also, and robed himself there to attend the service; the cardinals did not kneel at his benediction, as the people did, but acknowledged it with a profound inclination of the head.

On January 3rd, 1581, the Pope passed beneath our windows, and before him went some two hundred horses belonging to personages of the court, of one robe or the other. Close beside him was the Cardinal dei Medici, who conversed with him covered, and took him to his house to dinner. The Pope wore a red hat, a white garment, and a red velvet cowl, as is the habit. He was mounted on a white hackney, harnessed with red velvet, and with fringe and lace of gold. Though he was nearly eighty-one, he mounted without any aid, and every fifteen paces or so he gave his benediction. After him came three cardinals, and then some hundred men-at-arms, each with lance on thigh, and fully armoured save the head. They had in readiness also another hackney with like equipment, a mule, a handsome white

courser, and a litter.   Also two robe-
bearers with valises at their saddle-bows.

On January 11th, in the morning, as
M. de Montaigne was leaving the house
on horseback to go to the bank, he met
Catena,[1] a famous robber and banditti chief,
whom they were taking away from the
prison.   This man had raised a panic all
through Italy, monstrous tales of murder
being told about him ; notably concerning
two Capuchins, whom he forced to deny
God, and promised to spare their lives on
this condition.   But he slew them afterwards without any motive either of gain or
of vengeance.   M. de Montaigne halted to
behold the spectacle.   Over and beyond the
escort customary in France, they let precede

[1] *Essais,* ii. 11 : "Je me recontray un jour à Rome, sur
le poinct qu'on defaisoit Catena, un voleur insigne : on
l'étrangla sans ancune émotion de l'assistance, mais
quand on vint à le mettre à quartiers, le bourreau ne
donnoit coup, que le peuple ne suivist d'une voix
plaintive, et d'une exclamation, comme si chacun eust
presté son sentiment à cette charongue." Catena was
thirty years of age, and was charged with fifty-four
murders.

the criminal a huge crucifix draped with
black, at the foot of which went a great
crowd of men wearing cloaks and masks of
cloth, and these were said to be of the chief
gentlefolk of Rome, a confraternity sworn
to accompany criminals to execution and
corpses to the grave. Two of these—or
two monks in similar garb—helped the condemned man into the cart and preached to
him, one of them letting him kiss con-
tinually a picture of our Lord. This they
did so that those in the street might not see
the man's face. At the gibbet, which was a
beam upon two posts, they held this picture
before his face till he was thrown off the
ladder. He died as criminals commonly
do, without movement or cry; a dark man
of thirty or thereabout, and after he was
strangled they cut his body in four quarters.
It is the custom amongst these people to kill
criminals without torture, and after death to
subject the body to very barbarous usage.
M. de Montaigne remarked that he had
written elsewhere how deeply people are

moved by the cruelties practised upon dead bodies,[1] and on this occasion the crowd, who had not felt any pity at the hanging, cried out in lamentation at every stroke of the axe.   As soon as he was dead divers Jesuits or other churchmen went up to a high place and cried to the people on all sides that they should take to heart this example.

We remarked in Italy, and especially in Rome, that very few of the churches have clocks, there being fewer in Rome than in the meanest French village.   Also very few images are to be seen, save those made recently, several ancient churches being quite bare thereof.   On January 14th M. de Montaigne saw the execution of two brothers, formerly servants of the Castellan's secretary, who some days ago slew their master by night

---

[1] "Je conseillerois que ces exemples de rigueur, par le moyen ʃdesquels on veut tenir le peuple en office : s'exerçassent contre les corps des!criminels.   Car de les voir priver de ,sepulture, de les voir bouillir et mettre à quartiers, cela toucheroit quasi autant le vulgaire, que les peines qu'on fait souffrir aux vivans."—*Essais*, ii. 11.

in the palace of Signor Jacomo Buoncompagno, the Pope's son. Their flesh was torn
with pincers and their hands cut off, in front
of the aforesaid palace, and after this muti-
lation they put over the wounds the bodies
of capons which they had killed and cut
open just before.[1] This execution took
place on a scaffold, where the criminals
were first knocked down with heavy wooden
clubs, and then their throats were cut; it
is, so the report goes, a form of punish-
ment used in Rome from time to time,
but some held that it had been specially
appointed for this misdeed, for that the
criminals had killed their master in like
manner.

As to the bigness of Rome, M. de Montaigne declared that the space which the

[1] The employment of fowls in this connection was
generally curative. Pepys writes, in describing the
treatment of a half-drowned man (vol. vii. p. 288, ed.
1896), "and they did lay pigeons to his feet while I was
in the house, and all despair of him and with good
reason." In the case of these criminals the remedy may
have been applied to revive them for the next stage of
the torture.

walls enclose, more than a third thereof
being void, and the site of old and new
Rome as well, would equal an enclosure
made round Paris to take in all the fau-
bourgs.   But, reckoning the bulk of the
two cities by the number and closeness of the
houses and inhabitants, he deemed that
Rome would fall short of Paris by one-
third.   In number and grandeur of public
places, and in beauty of streets and palaces,
Rome seemed far superior.

He found the cold of winter little less
bitter than that of Gascony.   About Christmas there were sharp frosts and the wind
was intolerably cold; and after that it fre-
quently thundered, hailed, and lightened.
In the palaces the suites of apartments are
large, one room after the other, and you
may have to pass through three or four
rooms before you come to the chief saloon.
In certain houses where M. de Montaigne
dined in ceremony the buffet was not set
in the dining-room, but in one adjoining,
whither the servants would go to fetch drink

for whomsoever might call for it ; there too was displayed the silver plate.

On Thursday, January 26th, M. de Montaigne went to see the Janiculum Hill beyond the Tiber and the curiosities of that part ; amongst others a great fall of masonry from the old walls which had happened a few days before, and the view of the whole of Rome, which can be surveyed more clearly from this spot than from any other. Thence he went down to the Vatican to inspect the statues set in the niches of the Belvedere, and the fine gallery,[1] now almost completed, which the Pope is adorning with paintings of all parts of Italy. He lost his purse and all therein, and deemed this must have happened while he was giving alms—as he did twice or thrice ; the weather was very rainy and unpleasant, and, instead of returning his purse to his pocket, he must have thrust it into the slashing of his hose. At this time he diverted himself entirely in studying

[1] Probably the Sala Ducale, painted by Mattheus Bril.

Rome. He had at first engaged a Frenchman as guide, but this fellow took himself
off in some ridiculous humour, whereupon
M. de Montaigne prided himself on master-
ing by his own efforts the art of a guide.
In the evening he would study certain books
and maps, and next day repair to the spot
and put in practice his apprenticeship, so
that in a few days he could have shown his
guide the way.

M. de Montaigne affirmed that he could
now see nothing more of Rome than the
sky under which it lay and the area of its
site ; that all the knowledge he possessed
thereof was of an abstract and contemplative
nature, a knowledge in no way to be appre-
hended by the operation of the senses ; that
those who affirmed that they might at least
behold the ruins of Rome, affirmed too
much. The ruins of a mechanism of such
terrible power suggested to his own mind
reverence and respect rather than compre-
hension. What he saw was nought but a
sepulchre. The world, resentful at her long

domination, first broke and shattered all the portions of this marvellous whole, and then, horror-stricken at this spectacle of death, ruin, and disfigurement, entombed the ruins themselves. As to these minor indications of her overthrow which yet lie upon her bier, they have been preserved by fate as a testimony to that immeasurable greatness which all these centuries, all these conflagrations, all these repeated alliances of the powers of the world, have failed to destroy entirely. But it was almost certain that these defaced fragments which survived were those of the least merit, for the rage of the enemies of this immortal renown would surely have prompted them to destroy in the first instance all that was most lovely and most noble. He declared that the buildings of this bastard Rome, which were now being joined on to the ancient masonry (what though they sufficed to kindle the admiration of the present age), reminded him exactly of the nests the martins and crows were building in the roofs and on the walls of the French churches which the Huguenots had destroyed.[1]

Again M. de Montaigne was persuaded, considering the space occupied by this vast tomb, that the present age failed to realise its full extent, and that the greater part of the sepulchre itself must be buried. As to this, one has only to consider the base off-cast of a great city; how out of the fragments of broken tiles and pots from ancient days, a mound has been heaped together of so vast a size that it equals in height and breadth several natural mountains (he compared this mound as to height with the hill of Gurson, and judged it to be double the width).[2] It seemed to represent an express

[1] There had been considerable activity in the reconstruction of the city under Pius IV. The reigning Pope had continued this work as far as the disorder in the finances would permit. The most important building operations were carried out a little later under Sixtus V. —operations which were accompanied unfortunately by the destruction of many interesting remains of antiquity.

[2] Monte Testaccio. Gurson was a village in Périgord, the seat of the Marquis de Foix, an intimate friend of Montaigne.

decree of the Fates to make plain to the world
how they had conspired to render this city
glorious and paramount; to bear witness to
its grandeur by so strange and extraordinary
a token.   He declared it was hard to understand—considering how narrow was the space
occupied by some of the hills, and notably
by the most famous, the Capitol and the
Palatine—how such a large number of buildings could be there bestowed.   Looking only
at the remains of the Temple of Peace by
the side of the *Forum Romanum* (of which
one may still behold the recent ruin, like
that of a vast mountain broken up into
divers ugly crags), it was apparent that two
such edifices could hardly have found room
on the entire summit of the Capitol, where
there were twenty-five or thirty temples,
besides several private houses.   But in sooth
the various conjectures which have been
adopted for the delineation of this ancient
city possess scarcely any verisimilitude, seeing
that the very site thereof has changed its
contour beyond measure, and that certain

of its valleys have been filled up. To wit, in the lowest-lying spots, as, for instance, in the Velabrum, which, on account of its situation, received the sewage of the city, and had a lake in its midst, there is now to be found a hill as high as the other natural hills adjacent thereto.[1] All this has come about by the accumulation of the ruins and fragments of the huge buildings, the Monte Savello being nought else than a portion of the theatre of Marcellus. M. de Montaigne did not deem that an ancient Roman would recognise the site of his city were he to behold it.

It would often happen to one digging deep in the earth to come upon the capital of a lofty column which still stood on its base far below; and builders were wont to seek for their erections no other foundations than some mass of ancient masonry, or on arches such as are commonly seen in

[1] This is incorrect : the present position and aspect of the Temple of Janus indicate very little alteration of the level of the surface.

cellars, or on some old wall or substructure
existing on the site. And upon the very
wrecks of the ancient buildings, as they fall
to ruin, the builders set out casually the
foundations of new houses, as if these fragments were great masses of rock, firm and
trustworthy. It is evident that many of the
old streets lie more than thirty feet below
the level of those now in existence.

On January 28th M. de Montaigne had
colic, which, however, did not interfere with
his customary movements, and passed one
rather large stone and some small ones. On
the 30th he witnessed the most ancient religious ceremony that still subsists amongst
men—to wit, the circumcision of the Jews—
and gave most attentive and profitable atten-
tion thereto. He had already visited their
synagogue one Saturday morning, and heard
their prayers, when they sang in irregular
wise certain portions of the Hebrew Bible
suited to the occasion, after the manner of
the Calvinist churches. They are cadences
of similar sound, but the discord is excessive

by reason of the mixing together of voices of
all ages, for even the youngest children are
of the party, and all understand Hebrew but
indifferently.   They are no more attentive
to their prayers than we are, for they talk of
other things during their service, and exhibit
little reverence for their mysteries.   At the
entrance they wash their hands, and inside
they count it a curse to remove their headgear, but they do reverence, as their worship
ordains, by bowing and kneeling.   On the
shoulders or on the head they wear certain
pieces of linen decked with fringe; but to
describe these details would take too much
time.   After dinner their doctors give instruction by turns upon the passage of the
Bible for the day, speaking in Italian, and
next an assistant doctor selects one of the
hearers, or sometimes two or three in succession, to hold argument with the one who has
been teaching upon the subject of his discourse.   It seemed to M. de Montaigne that
the man we heard displayed great eloquence
and mental power in arguing his case.

But as to the circumcision itself, this ceremony takes place in the private house, the lightest and most convenient chamber thereof being chosen for the purpose. In this particular case, because the dwelling itself was ill suited therefor, the ceremony took place in the lobby by the door. As with us a godfather and a godmother are provided for the child, whom the father names, and the circumcision is performed the eighth day after birth. The godfather seats himself on a table with a pillow on his lap, and the godmother brings to him the child and then withdraws, the child being swaddled after our own fashion. The godfather then loosens the bandages below, and the assistants and the one whose duty it is to perform the operation all begin a chant and continue to sing during the operation, which takes about a quarter of an hour. He who officiates need not be a rabbi, and any one of them, whoever he may be, will be anxious to discharge this duty, because they hold that frequent bid-

ding to such a function is a great blessing:
nay, they will pay to be called in, offering
here a vestment and there something else
useful to the child. Moreover, they believe
that any one who may circumcise a particular
number of children will enjoy a certain
privilege after death, to wit, that the parts
about the mouth will never be eaten by
worms. On the table where the godfather
sits they forthwith lay out plentiful provision of all instruments necessary for this
operation, and in addition to these an
assistant holds in his hands a phial of wine
and a glass. There is also an earthen
brazier, at which the operator first warms
his hands; and then the child, with the
swaddling bands unloosed, is presented to
him by the godfather, who holds it in his
lap with the head towards himself. The
operator then takes hold of the part and
pulls forward the skin thereof with one
hand and with the other thrusts back the
fleshy substance and fixes a silver instrument
on the skin. This instrument, kept close

to the flesh within, holds the foreskin in proper position and prevents any injury to the other parts from the act of cutting. This done, he cuts off the skin and buries it at once in some earth, which along with other apparatus of the mystery is beside him, ready prepared in a basin, and then with his bare nails proceeds to remove any other particle of skin which may be left on the flesh. This operation is one requiring considerable skill and is somewhat painful, but it is quite free from danger and the wound is almost always healed after four or five days. The children cry as ours cry when they are baptized. As soon as the operation is done, the bystanders hand forthwith to the operator some wine, who, after having taken some of it into his mouth, sucks the bleeding flesh and then empties his mouth, repeating this act thrice. Then they give him in a wrap of paper red powder, which they call dragon's blood, and with this he dresses and covers the wound, and then binds up the same neatly with linen cut for the purpose. He is offered a glass full of wine which, according to report, he blesses by the words he speaks over it, and then drinks a mouthful. He next dips his finger in it and thrice lets the child suck some drops of wine therefrom. This glass they send as it is to the mother and the women of the family who are in some other part of the house, that they may finish the wine that remains. Then another, a third person, takes a silver instrument, made round like a tennis ball, with a long handle thereto, and pierced with little holes like our perfume boxes, and holds it first to the nose of the operator, next to the child, and last to the godfather. They believe that the odours therein help to strengthen and purify the soul for devotion. The operator meantime bears the stains of blood on his mouth.

On the 8th and on to the 12th M. de Montaigne had symptoms of colic and passed some stones, but without any great pain. This year, by the Pope's permission, greater liberty was given for the Carnival

everything being covered with pearls and jewels. Whenever they go abroad, whether in a coach or to a festivity or to the theatre, they keep apart from men : nevertheless in certain dances they mix freely enough, and find full opportunity of conversing and touching hands. The men on all occasions go clad very simply in black or Florentine serge, and are somewhat darker in skin than we are. I cannot say why they do not use their titles of duke, count, and marquis, when they have full right thereto, seeing that their appearance is somewhat ordinary. Otherwise they are most courteous, and as gracious as they can be, in spite of what is asserted by the baser sort of Frenchmen, who never find any gentility in those who resent their turbulence and insolent carriage. In every way we do our utmost to win a bad name, nevertheless the Italians nurse their ancient affection and reverence for France, which secures respect and welcome for all who deserve the same ever so little, and bear themselves without offence.

On the following Thursday he went to a feast given by the Castellan for which vast preparation had been made, notably an amphitheatre very artistically and sumptuously disposed for the sport of tilting, the courses being run in the evening before supper. The amphitheatre was erected in a square barn, a section, oval in form, having been set out in the centre for the purpose. Amongst other curious devices the floor was painted with the utmost despatch with certain designs in red. This floor had previously been covered with plaster, then they laid thereupon a piece of parchment or leather with designs according to their taste cut out of the same, and lastly they painted this with a brush dipped in red paint so as to leave on the plaster under the openings the design they wished for. So rapid was their work that they might easily have decorated the nave of a church in two hours. At supper the ladies were served by their husbands, who stood by them and gave them to drink and whatever they might ask for.

On the table were many roast fowls, their plumage having been restored to them to give them the look of living birds, capons cooked whole in vessels of glass, good store of hares, rabbits, and birds in pies with feathers as if alive, and the tables admirably laid with linen. The ladies' table, which was laid for four courses, could be removed in portions, and below the first service was a second one of sweetmeats ready prepared.

They use no masks for visiting one another, but they wear them, of a very cheap sort, when they walk about the town in public or go to meetings for running at the ring. On Carnival Monday two rich and well-appointed companies of gentlemen met for the sport aforesaid with a wealth of superb horses such as we cannot equal.

Having given leave of absence to the one of my followers who has up to this time written this journal in admirable fashion, I feel that, albeit it may irk me somewhat, I must needs continue the work with my own hand, seeing that it is so far advanced.

On February 16th, as I was returning from service, I saw in a small chapel a priest, fully robed, engaged in healing a man possessed, who was melancholic and apparently in a trance. They kept him kneeling before the altar, his neck being bound with some sort of cloth by which they held him fast. The priest recited in his presence many prayers and exorcisms out of his breviary, charging the devil to quit the body of this man;[1] then he addressed his discourse to the patient, speaking sometimes to the man himself and sometimes to the devil in his body, railing at him, dealing the poor wretch heavy blows with his fist, and spitting in his face. To these commands the patient made divers meaningless replies: now for himself, telling how he was affected by the operation of his malady; now for the devil, acknowledging his fear of God and the powerful

---

[1] Exorcism is still a portion of the baptismal rite in the Roman Church.

working of these exorcisms against him. After this performance, which lasted some time, the priest, by way of preparation for the final attack, withdrew to the altar and took in his left hand the pyx which held the *Corpus Domini*, and in his right a lighted candle, which he held upside down so that it might melt and consume away, saying certain prayers the while, and ending with threatenings and denunciations against the devil, · uttered in the loudest and most authoritative voice he could put forth. As soon as the first candle had burnt itself out close to his fingers, he took a second and then a third. He next put back the transparent vessel containing the *Corpus Domini*, and returned to the patient, speaking to him as to an ordinary man and releasing him from his bonds. He then delivered the patient over to his friends, and directed them to take him home.

The priest assured us that this devil was of the most noxious sort and very obstinate, and that his expulsion would prove a difficult task; moreover, he recounted to ten or twelve gentlemen who were present divers histories concerning this science of exorcism and his common experience thereof, notably how the day before he had cast out of a certain woman a great devil, who in leaving her had caused her to vomit from her mouth nails and pins and a bit of his hairy skin. And when her friends told him that she was not yet quite herself, he replied that this was because of another sort of spirit, easier to deal with and less malicious, who had taken possession of her this same morning. This kind (for he knew the names and the divisions and the minutest differences) was very easy to exorcise. But I saw no further proof of his skill. The man who had been under treatment gave no other facial sign than grinding his teeth and twisting his mouth when the *Corpus Domini* was put before him; he muttered, indeed, several times the words *Si fata volent*, for he was a notary and knew a word or two of Latin.

On the first day of March I went to the service at the Sistine Chapel. At the high altar the priest who said mass stood beyond the altar with his face turned towards the people, no one being behind him. On this occasion the Pope was present, for he had some days before excluded therefrom the nuns who had hitherto been wont to be present, so as to make more room. In their place he installed, by a most excellent regulation, the poor folk who beg about the city. Each one of the cardinals gave twenty crowns in aid of the movement, and very liberal alms were given by other private persons. To their hospital the Pope has given five hundred crowns a month.

In Rome there is a vast amount of private devotion, and many confraternities in which are manifest striking testimonies of piety, but it seems to me that in general there is less devotion than in the better ordered towns of France. They set more store here on ceremonies, in which they go to great lengths. Here I may write what I will with a free conscience, so I will give two illustrations of my meaning. A certain

man was with a courtesan, lying in bed and
enjoying the full liberty of the situation,
when, at the twenty-fourth hour, the *Ave
Maria* sounded, and the girl sprang out of
bed and knelt down on the floor to say her
prayer.   Shortly afterwards he was with
another, when suddenly the good mother
(for these girls are always in the hands of
some old bawd whom they call mother or
aunt) knocked at the door and, having
entered in a transport of rage, tore off from
the girl's neck a ribbon from which was
hanging a little image of Our Lady, so that
it might not be contaminated by the sinful
act of the wearer.   The young girl showed
herself exceedingly penitent, in that she had
omitted her customary practice of first removing this image from her person.

The ambassador of the Muscovite [1] was
present at this service, clad in a scarlet
mantle, a long coat of cloth of gold, and a
hat of cloth of gold made in the shape of
a nightcap and trimmed with fur, under

[1] Sent by Ivan the Terrible.

which was a smaller cap of cloth of silver.
This is the second ambassador of Muscovy
who has been sent to the papal court, the
other having come here in the time of Paul
III. Report said that this man's mission
was to stir up the Pope to interfere in the
war which the King of Poland was waging
against his master. His plea was that the
Muscovite ruler must needs sustain the first
onslaught of the Turk, and that, should he
be weakened by fighting Poland, he would
be unable to undertake war elsewhere, thus
leaving open a wide breach through which
the Turk might enter and attack us all.
The Muscovite also offered to make certain concessions in the religious controversies
at present pending between himself and
the Roman Church. The ambassador had
lodging with the Castellan, as had the other
in Pope Paul's time, and was maintained at
the Pope's charges. He resisted stiffly to
conform to the usage of kissing the Pope's
foot, consenting only to kiss his right hand,
and remained obstinate until it was pointed

out to him that even the Emperor was not exempt from this ceremonial duty, the instances of kings being insufficient to convince him. He could speak no language other than his own, and had come unaccompanied by an interpreter, and with only three or four men in his train. It is said he was in great peril as he journeyed in disguise through Poland. In his country there is such great ignorance of external affairs, that he took to Venice letters from his master addressed to the High Governor of the Signiory of Venice ; and, being asked what might be the meaning of this style, replied that in Muscovy they believed that Venice was under the command of the Pope, who sent thither governors, as he did to Bologna and other cities. God knows in what mood the Magnificoes must have listened to such ignorant discourse. Both to them and to the Pope he brought presents of sables, and of furs still more rich and rare, to wit, skins of the black fox.

On the 6th of March I went to see the

rary of the Vatican, which is contained
five or six rooms all communicating one
ith the other. There are many rows of
:sks, each desk having a great number of
ioks chained thereto. Also, in the chests,
hich were all opened for my inspection, I
w many manuscripts, of which I chiefly
marked a Seneca and the *Opuscula* of
lutarch. Amongst the noteworthy sights
saw was the statue of the good Aristides,[1]
ith a fine head, bald and thickly bearded,
grand forehead, and an expression full of
reetness and majesty. The base is very
cient, and has his name written thereupon.
iaw likewise a Chinese book writ in strange
aracters, on leaves made of a certain stuff
uch more tender and transparent than
e paper we use, and because this fabric is
it thick enough to bear the stain of ink,
ey write on only one side of the sheet,
d the sheets are all doubled and folded at

This was not the Athenian, but Ælius Aristides, a
:torician of Smyrna, who lived in the time of M.
relius. The inscription on the pedestal is ΑΡΙΣΤΙΔΕΣ
ITPΣEOΣ.

the outside edges by which they are held
together.   It is said that these sheets are
the bark of a certain tree, as is a fragment
of ancient papyrus which I saw covered with
unknown characters.   I saw also the Breviary
of Saint Gregory in manuscript, which has
no date, but the account they give of it
states that it has come down from one hand
to another from Saint Gregory's time.   It
is a missal not unlike our own, and it was
taken to the recent Council at Trent as an ˅
authority for the ceremonies of our Church.
Next, a book by Saint Thomas Aquinas, containing corrections made by the author himself, who wrote badly, using a small character ˅
worse even than my own.   Next, a Bible
printed on parchment, one of those which
Plantin [1] has recently printed in four languages, which book King Philip presented
to the Pope, according to an inscription on
the cover.   Next, the original manuscript of
the book which King Henry of England

[1] The polyglot version printed by the famous Antwerp
Press in 1569.

wrote against Luther and sent fifty years
ago to Pope Leo X.[1] It contains a sub-
scription and a graceful Latin distich, both
written by his own hand :—

> " Anglorum Rex Henricus, Leo decime, mittit
>   Hoc opus, & fidei testem & amicitæ."

I read both the prefaces, one to the Pope
and the other to the reader. The king
claims indulgence for any literary shortcom-
ings on the score of his military occupations,
but the style is good scholastic Latin. I
inspected the library without any difficulty ;
indeed, any one may visit it and make what
extracts he likes; it is open almost every
morning. I was taken to every part thereof
by a gentleman, who invited me to make use
of it as often as I might desire.

Our ambassador quitted Rome just at this
time without having ever seen the library,
and he complained because pressure had been

---

[1] Assertio septem sacramentorum. It was presented
to the Pope by the English Ambassador in 1521. The
scansion of the couplet is not perfect.

put upon him to beg this favour of Cardinal Charlet,[1] and that he had never been allowed to inspect the manuscript Seneca, which he desired greatly to see. It was my good luck which carried me on to success, for, having heard of the ambassador's failure, I was in despair. Thus it seems all things come easily to men of a certain temper, and are unattainable by others. Right occasion and opportunity have their privileges, and often hold out to ordinary folk what they deny to kings. Curiosity often stands in its own way, and the like may be affirmed of greatness and power. In the library I saw also a manuscript Virgil[2] in an exceedingly large handwriting, of that long and narrow character which we see in Rome in inscriptions of the age of the Emperors somewhere about the reign of Constantine, a character which takes somewhat of Gothic form, and

[1] Cardinal Sirleto, one of the most learned and benevolent men of the age. He was the tutor of Carlo Borromeo. He died in 1585, and lies buried in S. Lorenzo. Ranke, i. 347.

[2] Probably the Codex Romanus of the fifth century.

misses that square proportion which the old
Latin inscriptions possess.   The sight of this
Virgil confirmed a belief which I have always
held, to wit, that the four lines usually put
at the opening of the Æneid are borrowed,
since this copy has them not.   Also a copy
of the Acts of the Apostles, written in very
fair Greek golden character.   The lettering
is massive, solid in substance, and raised upon
the paper, so that any one who may pass his
finger over the same will detect the thickness
thereof.   We have, I believe, lost all knowledge of this method.

On March 13th an old Antiochan patriarch,
an Arabian, and well versed in five or six of
the languages of those regions, and quite
ignorant of Greek or of the other tongues
we use, a personage with whom I had become very intimate, gave me a certain com-
pound for the relief of my gravel, and written
directions for the employment of the same.
He bestowed it for me in a little earthen
pot, where I might keep it ten or even twenty
years, and assured me that I might anticipate

a complete cure of my distemper by the first
dose I should take.   In case I might lose the
writing he gave me, I will set down his in-
structions here.   The drug should be taken
at bedtime after a light supper ; a piece the
size of two peas should be mixed in lukewarm water, after having been crumbled in
the fingers.   This will make five doses, one
to be taken every alternate day.

· One day I dined with our ambassador at
Rome, where Muret[1] and other learned men
were of the company.   I spoke concerning the
translation of Plutarch into French, and con-
troverted those who esteem it less than I do.
I maintained at least that, in passages where
the translator may have missed the exact
meaning of Plutarch, he has given instead
one verisimilar and in accurate combination

[1] Marc-Antoine Muret, a learned Frenchman, who
passed many years in Italy.   Montaigne mentions him,
Essais, i. 25 : "Et Nicolas Grouchi, qui a escrit *De Comitiis
Romanorum*, Guillaume Guerente, qui a commenté
Aristote ; George Bucanan, ce grand Poëte Escossois ;
Marc-Antoine Muret (que la France et l'Italie recog-
noist pour le meilleur orateur du temps), mes precepteurs
domestiques. . . ."

with what is writ before and after. To show
me that I was hereby claiming too much for
this work, they brought forward two passages; one (the criticism of which they
assigned to a son of M. Mangot,[1] a Parisian
advocate, who had just quitted Rome) was
from the life of Solon—somewhere about
the middle—in which the translator says that
Solon claimed for himself that he had given
freedom to Attica, and had removed the
boundary stones which divided inherited plots
of land. Here he had made a mistake, for
the Greek word in question[2] is rather used to
denote certain signposts which were wont to
be set up on lands which were pledged or
under bond, so that buyers might be fore-

---

[1] This is almost certainly an allusion to Claude
Mangot, a French jurisconsult, who died in 1579, and
left two sons. (A.)

[2] Ὅρος. The passage runs: Ὅρους ἀνεῖλε πολλαχῇ
πεπηγότας πρόσθεν δὲ δουλεύουσα νῦν ἐλεύθερα. Amyot's
rendering is, "Car il se vante & glorifie en ses vers
d'avoir osté toutes les bornes qui paravant faisoient les
separations des heritages en tout le territoire de l'Attique
laquelle il dit avoir affranchie au lieu que paravant elle
estoit serue."

warned that these were mortgaged. The word which the translator employed has none of the meaning of the original, inasmuch as it would lead the reader to infer that the lands alluded to were not separate freeholds, but were held in common. The Latin of Estienne comes nearer to the truth.[1] The second passage was one near the end of the treatise on the " Nurture of Children." This the translator gives as follows : " The observation of these rules is rather to be desired than advised." But his critics now affirmed the real meaning of the Greek to be : " That thing is more to be desired than to be hoped for." The same proverb may be found elsewhere under different form. In place of this clear and intelligible meaning the translator has substituted one which is weak and foreign. Wherefore, accepting their presupposition of the true sense of the passage

[1] Maxima pars novis tabulis aiunt semel fuisse pacta conventa universa circumducta quibus consonare citius carmina Solonis. Gloriatur etiam in his agri se ante pignori nexi fixos passim terminos removisse, quæ pridem serviebant, nunc libera esse.

in question, I professed myself entirely of
their opinion.[1]

In Rome the churches are inferior to those
of the generality of the large towns of Italy ;
indeed, speaking generally of Italy and Germany, the churches will rarely be found to
equal those of France. At Saint Peter's, at
the door of the new church, are to be seen
certain flags draped as trophies, bearing inscriptions which tell that they are ensigns
captured by the king from the Huguenots,
but these inscriptions do not say where
or when. Near to the Gregorian Chapel,
where may be seen attached to the wall
a vast number of *ex votos*, there is a
small square picture, wretched and badly
painted, which represents the battle of
Moncontour. In the hall, in front of the
Sistine Chapel,[2] or upon the partition wall,

[1] Montaigne's frank acceptance of this censure on
Amyot, whom he held in the highest esteem, is a remarkable instance of his liberality of mind.

[2] The Sala Regìa adjoining the Sistine Chapel. The
frescoes representing the fleet of Don John and the
battle of Lepanto are by Vasari ; who likewise painted

ISLAND ON THE TIBER

are several paintings of memorable events touching the Holy See—for instance, the sea fight of Don John of Austria; also a representation of that Pope who trod under foot the head of the Emperor when he came to entreat pardon and to kiss the Pope's feet; but on the same is no trace of the words which according to history were spoken by each one of them. There are two other pictures which accurately represent the wounding and the death of the Admiral of Chatillon.

On March 15th M. de Monluc[1] came to me at daybreak, and we set about the execution of the plan which we had made the day previous to go to see Ostia. We crossed the Tiber by the bridge of Our Lady, and

the scenes of the massacre of S. Bartholomew and the murder of Coligny. The meeting of Pope Alexander and Frederic Barbarossa is by Giuseppe Porta.

[1] There is some uncertainty as to the identity of this person. The Marshal Blaise de Monluc, Montaigne's friend, died in 1577, his brother Jean in 1579, and in the *Essais*, ii. 8, he notices the death of Pierre, a son of the Marshal, in 1568. The passage may refer to a son of the Marshal.

left the city by the *Porta del Porto*, anciently
called *Portuensis*, and thence we followed a
rough road through a region only moderately productive of wine and corn. Having
gone about eight miles and once more struck
the bank of the Tiber, the road descended
into a vast plain of meadow and pasturage,
at the end of which stood formerly a large
town. Of this some fine and stately ruins
may yet be seen on the shore of the Lake of
Trajan, which is itself an overflow of the
Tyrrhenian sea, and was in ancient times
navigable for ships, but now very little sea-
water finds its way thereinto, and still less
into another lake a little above it, which
they call the Arch of Claudius.[1]

We might have taken our dinner with the
cardinal of Perugia, who was residing there.[2]
In sooth there is nothing anywhere to equal

[1] An obvious misprint for the Port of Claudius.

[2] At Porto. Fulvio della Cornia, a native of Perugia,
and a nephew of Julius III. He was deprived and imprisoned by Paul IV., who suspected him of favouring
the Spanish interests; but the reigning Pope had
advanced him to the bishopric of Porto.

the courtesy of the gentlefolk of these parts, and of their dependents. The cardinal aforesaid sent word to me by one of my servants who had passed by his house that he has some cause of complaint against me, in that I had not called upon him, this servant having been taken for refreshment into the cardinal's pantry; the cardinal had no acquaintance with me, and in this case was only showing the hospitality he was wont to give to strangers of any mark. On my part I heard that the day would hardly be long enough to allow us to complete the round I wished to make, seeing that I had gone many miles out of my way in order to get a sight of both banks of the Tiber. Here we crossed in a boat over a small branch of the Tiber to the Sacred Isle, a good Gascon league in length, where we found plenty of grazing land and divers ruins and columns of marble, which are abundant in all the parts about Porto, where stood the ancient city built by Trajan. Every day something of the kind is dug up by the Pope's workmen and sent to Rome. When we had crossed this island we found we had still the Tiber to pass, and, as we had no means of transporting our horses, we were just thinking of retracing our steps, when, by good luck, we espied on the opposite bank M. de Bellai, M. le Baron de Chasai, M. de Marivau, and certain others. Whereupon I crossed the stream and made an arrangement with these gentlemen that we should exchange horses. Thus they returned to Rome by the road by which we had come out, and we took theirs, which led direct to Ostia.

Ostia,[1] fifteen miles from Rome, is situated by the ancient channel of the Tiber, for this stream has changed its course somewhat, and is receding still more every day. We breakfasted in haste at a mean tavern, beyond which we could see La Rocca, a

---

[1] Ostia, though already in decay, was not in Montaigne's time the wretched place it is at present. La Rocca is possibly the castle built by San Gallo for Julius II. At Castel Fusano, a mile to the south, is one of the watch-towers alluded to, with stone figures of soldiers on the roof.

small castle strong enough in itself, but now
bare of a garrison. The Popes, and notably the present one, have built along this
coast high towers or look-outs, about a mile
apart, to guard against the raids often
made by the Turks, especially in the vintage
season, and the capture of men and cattle.
By the discharge of a cannon from these
towers they advise one another so rapidly
that the alarm is sped to Rome forthwith.
Round Ostia are the salt works, situated in
a wide marshy plain into which the sea
flows, and these supply all the States of the
Church.[1]   This road from Ostia to Rome,
the *Via Ostensis*, abounds in vestiges of its
ancient splendour, such as causeways and
ruins of aqueducts; moreover, all along it
is set with mighty ruins, and for two-thirds
of its length it is still paved with those
large black squares of stone which they
used formerly as pavement.   In looking at
this bank of the Tiber it is easy to believe

---

[1] The salt works of Ostia are said to go back to the
time of Ancus Martius.

that of old the road all the way from Rome
to Ostia ran past the habitations of men.
Amongst other ruins we saw, about midway
and on our left, a very beautiful tomb of
a Roman prætor with an inscription quite
perfect thereon. In Rome, the ruins, as a
rule, only manifest themselves to us by the
massive solidity of their construction. The
ancients built thick walls of brick, and these
they lined either with strips of marble or
some other white stone, or with a kind of
cement, or with thick tiles set thereupon.
This outside crust, on which the inscriptions were written, has almost everywhere
been ruined by the lapse of years, wherefore
we have now but little knowledge as to
all these matters. Inscriptions still remain
where the walls were originally built in
solid fashion.

The approaches to Rome in almost every
case have a barren and uncultivated look,
whether through the unfitness of the soil
for cultivation, or whether, as seems more
likely, through the absence of husbandmen

and handicraftsmen in the city. On my
journey hither I met divers troops of
villagers from the Grisons and Savoy on
their way to seek work in the Roman vineyards and gardens, and they told me they
gained this wage every year. The city is
all for the court and the nobility, every one
adapting himself to the ease and idleness
of ecclesiastic surroundings. There are no
main streets of trade; what there are would
seem small in a small town, palaces and
gardens take up all the space. Nothing is
to be seen like the Rue de la Harpe or de
Saint Denis; I always fancied I must be
walking in the Rue de Seine or on the
Quai des Augustins at Paris. The aspect
of the city differs little whether the day be
a feast or a working day. Services go on
all through Lent, and the crowds are just
as great on a working day as any other, the
streets being full of coaches, prelates, and
ladies at this season.

On the 16th of March, after our return
to Rome, I was taken to make trial of the

Roman hot baths at St. Mark's, which have
the best repute. I underwent a treatment
of moderate strength, and, though I went
alone, met with all possible respect. The
usual custom is to take a lady as companion,
who like yourself will be rubbed by the
men in attendance. I learned here the com-
position of the unguent used for removing
hair from the skin. It is made of two parts
of quick lime and one of arsenic, blended
with lye, and will have effect in less than a
quarter of an hour after application. On
the 17th I was troubled, not insupportably,
with colic for five or six hours, and afterwards passed a large stone the shape of a
pine kernel.

At this season we had roses and artichokes
as well, but the heat, according to my judgment, was not excessive. I wore the same
clothes as I wear at home. We got less fish
than in France ; their pike is a useless beast,
and is reckoned poor man's diet. Soles and
trout are rarely seen, but the sea barbel are
very good and much larger than at Bordeaux,

albeit dear. John Dorys and mullets, larger and less firm than ours, are very costly. The oil is so good that I never feel that irritation of the throat which always troubles me in France when I have partaken generously of it. Here you may eat grapes all the year round, and even up to this date fine bunches may be seen hanging on the trellises. The mutton is worthless and is in no esteem.

On the 18th the Portuguese ambassador did homage to the Pope for the kingdom of Portugal, on behalf of King Philip. This same ambassador represented on other occasions the late King of Portugal, and likewise those states of King Philip with which he was at variance.[1] On my way back from Saint Peter's I met a certain man who gave me an interesting account of two occurrences.

[1] On the death of Henry the Cardinal, in 1580, there was a disputed succession in Portugal, and Philip II. of Spain succeeded in taking possession of the kingdom. The states alluded to are, no doubt, the Low Countries. The name of the ambassador was Don Juan Gomez de Silva.

The first was that the Portuguese had done
their homage in Passion week, the service
being held in the church of Saint John at
the Porta Latina ; and the second, that in
this very same church, several years ago,
certain Portuguese had established a very
strange confraternity. These were men who
joined themselves in matrimony, using the
mass and the same religious ceremonies as
we use at our weddings, taking the sacrament
together, and reading our marriage service.
Then they went and lived together after
the fashion of married folk. These fanatics
declared that the marriage ceremony alone
rendered lawful the union of man and woman,
and that their own form of union would become equally lawful should it be sanctioned by
the ceremonies and mysteries of the Church.
Nine or ten Portuguese belonging to this exe-
crable sect were burnt.[1]

[1] Sono stati presi undeci fra Portoghesi et Spagnuoli, i
quali adunatisi in una chiesa ch'è vicina San Giovanni
Laterano, facevano alcune lor cerimonie, et con horrenda
scelleragine bruttando il sacrosanto nome di matrimonio
si maritavano l'un con l'altro, congiongendosi insieme

I witnessed the homage done by Spain for
the kingdom of Portugal.   A salvo of artil-
lery was fired from Saint Angelo and from
the palace, and the ambassador was escorted
by trumpets and drums and the Pope's archers.
I did not go inside to be present at the speech-
making and the other ceremonies. The Muscovite ambassador, who sat at a decorated
window to behold the procession, remarked
that he had been brought there to witness
a great gathering; but in his country, when
men spoke of troops of horses, they had in
mind twenty-five or thirty thousand, wherefore he made light of the show before him.
This I heard from a gentleman who was sent
to converse with him through an interpreter.
On Palm Sunday, in a church where I went
for vespers, I saw a child seated in a chair
beside the altar clad in a long gown of new
blue taffetas, bareheaded, crowned with olive

come marito con moglie.   Vintesette si trovavano et
più insieme, il più delle volte: ma questa volta non
ne hanno potuto coglier più che questi undici, i quali
anderanno al fuoco et come meritano.—Tiepolo, *Relazioni
Ven.*, August 2, 1578.

branches, and holding in his hand a lighted candle of white wax. This boy was about fifteen years old, and had just been discharged by the Pope's order from prison, having been sent there for killing another boy. At Saint John Lateran they showed me some transparent marble.

On the next day the Pope visited the seven churches.[1] He wore boots of flesh - colour, with a cross of lighter-coloured leather upon each boot. He always takes with him a Spanish horse, a hackney, a mule, and a litter, all equipped in the same fashion, but to-day the horse was lacking. His esquire, with two or three pairs of gilded spurs in his hand, awaited him at the foot of Saint Peter's Stairs; but he put the spurs aside and asked for his litter, in which were hanging two red hats of the same sort.

This evening they brought back to me the volume of my Essays, castigated and brought

[1] The pilgrimage churches: S. Giovanni in Laterano, S. Pietro, S. Paolo, S. Lorenzo, S. Maria Maggiore, S. Croce in Gerusalemme, and S. Sebastiano. The first five were the original patriarchal churches.

into harmony with the opinions of the monk-
ish doctors.   The *Maestro del Sacro Palazzo*
could only pronounce judgment on them
from the report of a certain French monk,
for he himself was ignorant of our language;
but he was so fully satisfied with the explana-
tions I gave him of all those passages to which
exception had been taken by the Frenchman,
that he left to me the task of correcting, according to my conscience, everything which
might appear wanting in good taste.   In return I begged him to follow the advice of the
censor of my book, and I avowed that in certain
matters—for instance, in my use of the word
Fortune [1] in discoursing on heretical poets; in
my apology for Julian; [2] in my remark that
when a man prays he ought for the time to
be free of all vicious inclinations; in certain
statements that it is cruelty to inflict upon ⌄
men greater pain than is necessary to kill
them; that children should be brought up to

---

[1] *Essais*, i. 33, has for title, *La fortune se rencontre
souvent au train de la raison.*

[2] *Essais*, ii. 19.

examine all sides of a question ; [1] and in many others—I did not admit I was in error. Moreover, in certain additional instances, I denied that my critic had caught my meaning. The aforesaid Maestro, who was a man of parts, completely exonerated me, and was anxious to let me see that he set small value on these emendations; moreover, he argued very ingeniously on my behalf against another man, an Italian, who was opposed to me. They kept back my copy of "The History of the Swiss," translated into French,[2] simply because they had found out that the translator was a heretic, though his name did not appear anywhere in the volume. It is wonderful what a wide knowledge they have of men and foreign lands, and the most singular part of it was they told me the preface of the aforesaid book was condemned.

This same day at the church of Saint John Lateran, in place of the ordinary

[1] *Essais*, i. 25.
[2] Probably, *La république des Suisses*, by Simler : Paris, 1578.

penitancers who may be seen doing their
office in most of the churches, Monsignore
the Cardinal of Saint Sixtus[1] sat in a
corner, and with a long rod, which he held
in his hand, touched the heads of all the
men who went by, and of the women also,
but these he regarded with a smile and a
courtesy of manner apportioned to their consequence and beauty.

On the Wednesday in Holy week I visited
the Seven Churches with M. de Foix[2] before
dinner and spent about five hours in making

[1] Filippo Buoncompagni, a nephew of the Pope. He
was born in 1548, died in 1581, and lies buried in S. Maria
Maggiore.

[2] Paul de Foix. He began his career in the magistracy ;
and, having fallen under suspicion of favouring the
Huguenots, was imprisoned by Henry II. He was re-
leased by the influence of Catherine dei Medici, and sent
on diplomatic missions to England and Venice. Under
Henry III. he entered the Church and became archbishop of Toulouse. He died in Rome in 1584. There
is mention of him in *Essais*, iii. 9. "Cette perte (of
M. de Pibrac) et celle qu'en mesme temps nous avons
faite de Monsieur de Foix, sont pertes importantes à
nostre couronnes. Je ne sçay s'il reste à la France de
quoy substituer une autre couple, pareille à ces deux
Gascons."

the round. I know not why some people should profess to be shocked when they hear this or that prelate accused of vicious practices, when these practices are well known. This very day, in the churches of Saint John Lateran and of Santa Croce in Gerusalemme, I saw written in a most prominent place the history of Pope Sylvester II.[1] in which the worst is recorded of him. The circuit of the city from the Porta del Popolo to the Porta de S. Paolo, which I made several

[1] The romantic story of this Pope is well known. Gerbert was an Auvergnat, a youth of great promise, and after studying at the Cluniac school of Avrillac, and under the Arabic teachers at Cordova, he became a teacher in the school at Reims. He became archbishop in 991 and for a time enjoyed the favour of Hugh Capet, but in 996 he fled to the imperial court and accompanied Otho III. to Italy in 998, being created archbishop of Ravenna at once, and elected Pope as Silvester II. in the following year. He died in 1003.

The myths which gathered round Silvester's personality are fully set forth by William of Malmesbury, and by Vincentius Bellovicensis in the *Speculum Historiale*. Having won the heart of his Arabian master's daughter, he stole his books and fled, helped on, it is hinted, by the devil, who was anxious that he should be preserved and sit in the chair of Peter. Like Friar Bacon, he made a brazen head with power of speech, and besides this a

times, can be accomplished in three or four hours going at foot pace. That part which lies beyond the river may easily be traversed in an hour and a half. Amongst other pleasures which I enjoyed in Rome during Lent, mention must be made of the sermons. There were many excellent preachers, for instance the renegade rabbi who preached to the Jews on Saturday afternoons in the church of the Trinità. Here was always a congregation of sixty Jews who were bound to be present. This preacher had been a

clock and a musical instrument which worked by steam. The head aforesaid prophesied that he would become Pope, and would die in Jerusalem, a prediction which was held to be fulfilled by the fact that he died after performing mass at Santa Croce in Gerusalemme. The belief in his unlawful knowledge was widespread and persistent, and in the *Vitæ Pontific. Ravennat.* it is written, *Homagium diabolo fecit et male finivit.*

It is strange that Montaigne, with his mind always sceptical of the marvellous, should have been led to regard Silvester's character in a sinister light. He had evidently read the laudatory epitaph in S. John Lateran written by Sergius IV., but he seems to have been inclined rather to credit the fables of the inscription in Santa Croce in Gerusalemme. The epitaph of Pope Sergius runs as follows :—

famous doctor amongst them, and now he
attacked their belief by their own arguments,

✠ ISE LOCUS MUNDI SILVESTRI MEMBRA SEPULTI
  VENTURO DOMINO CONFERET AD SONITUM
QUEM DEDERAT MUNDO CELEBRE DOCTISSIMA VIRGO
  ATQ. CAPUT MUNDI CULMINA ROMULEA
PRIMUM GERBERTUS MERUIT FRANCISGENA SEDE
  REMENSIS POPULI METROPOLIM PATRIÆ
INDE RAVENNATIS MERUIT CONSCENDERE SUMMUM
  ÆCCLESIÆ REGIMEN NOBILE SITQ : POTENS
POSTANNUM ROMAM MUTATO NOMINE SUMPSIT
  UT TOTO PASTOR FIERET ORBE NOVUS
CUI NIMIUM PLACUIT SOCIALE MENTE FIDELIS
  OBTULIT HOC CÆSAR TERTIUS OTTO SIBI
TEMPUS UTERQ : COMIT CLARA VIRTUTE SOPHIÆ
  GAUDET ET OMNE SECLUM FRANGITUR ROME REU
CLAVIGERI INSTAR ERAT CÆLORUM SEDE POTITUS
  TERNA SUFFECTUS CUI VICEPASTOR ERAT
ISE VICEM PETRI POSTQUAM SUSCEPIT ABEGIT
  LUSTRALI SPATIO SECULA MORTE SUI
OBRIGUIT MUNDUS DISCUSSA PACE TRIUMPHUS
  ÆCCLESIÆ NUTANS DEDIDICIT REQUIEM
SERGIUS HUNC LOCULUM MITI PIETATE SACERDOS
  SUCCESSORQ. SUUS COMPSIT AMORE SUI
QUISQUIS ADHUC TUMULUM DEVEXA LUMINA VERTIS
  OMNIPOTENS DOMINE DIC MISERERE SUI
OBIIT ANNO DOMINI CE INCARNATIONIS MIII INDIC
    I. M AI. Ð. XII.

The inscription in S. Croce in Gerusalemme has been
removed. It seems to have been *in situ* in 1592, as
it is referred to in Schrader's *Monumentorum Italiæ
Descriptio*, published that same year.

even out of the mouths of their rabbis and
from the words of the Bible.   He had
admirable skill and knowledge of the subject, and of the languages necessary for
the elaboration of the same.   There was
another who preached before the Pope and
cardinals, named Padre Toledo, a man of
extraordinary ability in depth of learning, in
appositeness of expression, and in mustering
of his arguments, and a third who preached
at the church of the Jesuits was distinguished for the beauty of the language he
used, the two last being members of the
Jesuit society.

It is wonderful how great is the part
occupied by this College in the Christian
economy, and my belief is that never before
has there existed any confraternity which
has risen to such eminence, or which may
sway so powerfully the destinies of the
world, supposing that it should be able to
prosecute its designs in the future.   It
occupies well-nigh the whole of Christen-
dom ; it is a nursery of men distinguished

in every department of high affairs, and the institution of our Church which the heretics of our day have most to fear.

One of the preachers declared that people nowadays use their coaches as places whence they spy upon their fellows. The habit which the Romans most affect is that of walking about the streets, but as a rule they only rouse themselves to issue forth for the sake of sauntering along from one street to another, without design of going anywhere in particular, one or two of the streets being especially affected for this purpose. In sooth, the chief pleasure to be got from this practice is the sight of the ladies, and especially the courtesans, who exhibit themselves behind their lattices with such refinement of trickery that I have often wondered at the address they display in attracting men's eyes. Often I have got down from my horse and induced some of these ladies to admit me, and have wondered how it was they contrived to make themselves appear

so much handsomer than they really were.[1]
They have the art of letting a beholder
distinguish them by whatever trait of theirs
is most seemly; they will let you see only
the upper part of the face, or the lower, or
the side, veiling and unveiling according to
the particular style of countenance, so that
an ugly woman is never to be seen at a
window. Each one takes her position there
for the purpose of saluting and bowing to

[1] *Essais*, ii. 15 : "Voyez en Italie, où il y a plus de
beaulté à vendre, et de la plus fine, comment il fault
qu'elle cherche d'aultres moyens estrangiers et d'aultres
arts pour se rendre agréable." Also *Essais*, iii. 5 : "Ils
font les poursuyvants en Italie et les transis de celles
mesmes qui sont à vendre ; et se deffendent ainsi : Qu'il
y a des degrez en la jouissance, et que par des services
il veulent obtenir pour eulx celle qui est la plus entière :
elles ne vendent que le corps : la volonté ne peult estre
mise en vente, elle est trop libre et trop sienne."

Madame Le Brun writes of a similar fashion at the end
of the eighteenth century : "On les voit à leur fenêtres
coiffées avec des fleurs, des plumes, fardées de rouge et
de blanc : le haut de leur corsage, que l'on aperçoit,
annonce une forte grande parure ; en sorte qu'un
amateur novice, qui veut faire connaissance avec elles,
est tout surpris, quand il entre dans leurs chambres,
de les trouver seulement vêtues d'un jupon sale."—
Souvenirs (Paris).

her acquaintances, who, as they go by, throw up many a glance. An extra privilege, granted to any gallant who may have paid one crown or four for passing the night in a house of this character, is that he is allowed to salute his inamorata in public the next day. Many ladies of quality also show themselves, but it is very easy to perceive that these are of totally different carriage and fashion. This phase of life is best seen from horseback, a usage which is followed by poor wretches like myself, or by young men riding great horses, which they manage with much skill. People of quality never go abroad except in coaches of the most costly sort, and, in order to have a clear view upwards, the roofs of the coaches are fitted with small windows. It was to these windows that the preacher aforesaid alluded when he spoke of the spying which went on in coaches.

On the morning of Holy Thursday the Pope, in pontifical garb, accompanied by the cardinals, repaired to the second platform of the great portico of Saint Peter's bearing a lighted torch in his hand. Then a canon of Saint Peter's, who stood on one side of the balcony, read in a loud voice a bull written in Latin by which men of an infinite variety of sorts and conditions were excommunicated; amongst others the Huguenots were specially named, and all those princes who keep hold on any of the lands of the Church, an article which caused loud laughter from the Cardinals Medici and Carafa, who stood close to the Pope. The reading of this bull lasted a good hour; for when the canon had finished reading an article in Latin, the Cardinal Gonzaga, who stood on the opposite side — uncovered like the canon — would repeat the same in Italian. When the reading was done the Pope cast the lighted torch down amongst the people; and, whether out of jest or not, Cardinal Gonzaga threw down another, three torches having been kindled. This having fallen amongst the people caused a vast disturbance below, every one scrambling to pick up a fragment of the torch, and giving and taking shrewd blows with fist or cudgel. During the reading of this sentence the balustrade of the portico in front of the Pope was covered with a large piece of black taffetas; but, the excommunication having been pronounced, they folded up this black covering and disclosed one of a different colour, whereupon the Pope gave his public blessing.

On these days they exhibit the handkerchief of Saint Veronica. This is a countenance wrought in needlework, of a dark and sombre tint, and framed after the fashion of a mirror. It is shown with great ceremony from a high pulpit, five or six paces in width, and the priest who holds it wears on his hands red gloves, while two or three other priests assist him in displaying it. No spectacle provokes such great show of reverence as this, the people all prostrate themselves on the ground, the greater part of them weeping and uttering cries of pity. A woman, whom they declared to be possessed, made a great uproar at the sight of this effigy, and began to screech, and twist her arms, and throw them about. The priests moved round the pulpit and exhibited the effigy, now from one side and now from another, and at every fresh display the people who beheld it cried out aloud. On these same occasions they show to the people likewise with equal cere- monies a lance head enclosed in a crystal vessel. This display is made several times during the day, and the crowd which comes to witness the same is so vast that, as far as the eye can reach from the pulpit aforesaid outside the church, there is nought to be seen but an endless crowd of men and women. Here is the true papal court; the pomp of Rome and its chief grandeur lies in the outward show of religion : and it is a fine sight in these days, this unbounded ardour of the people for their faith.

In the city a hundred or more confraterni- ties are to be found, and almost every gentle- man is a member of some one of these : some of them are open to strangers, and our kings of France belong to that of the Gonfalon.

Each particular society is wont to exercise, and especially during Lent, certain functions of religious fellowship, and on this special day they walk about in companies clad in linen gowns, each company wearing its particular colour, white, red, blue, green, or black, almost all with their faces covered. The most striking sight I ever saw here or elsewhere was the incredible number of people spread abroad through the city this day, busy with their devotions, and especially those belonging to the aforesaid confraternities. For, in addition to the great crowds seen during the day round about Saint Peter's, the whole city, as night approached, seemed to be on fire on account of the procession of these confraternities towards Saint Peter's, each one bearing a lighted candle — almost always of white wax — in his hand. I am sure that at least twelve thousand torches must have gone by the place where I stood ; for, from eight o'clock till midnight, the street was filled with the procession, marshalled and regulated in such excellent order that, though there were many different companies coming from different places, the ranks were never broken or the progress stayed. Each confraternity had a fine choir of musicians, who sang as they marched. In the midst of the ranks went a file of penitancers to the number of five hundred, who scourged themselves with cords, and left their backs all raw and bloody. This is a riddle which still baffles me, but there is no denying that they were bruised and wounded in cruel fashion, and that this self-torture and flagellation went on without ceasing. Judging by the aspect of their faces, the assurance of their gait, and the steadfastness audible in their discourse and visible in their countenances (for I heard several of them speak, and many uncovered themselves in passing through the street), it would never have suggested itself to me that they were engaged in a painful and irksome task. Amongst them were youths of twelve or thirteen years of age, and right in front of me was one, very young and fair in

seeming, over whose wounds a young woman
lamented sore; but the boy, turning towards
us, said with a laugh, "Enough of that;
what I do I do for your sins and not for my
own." [1] Not only was there absent all appearance of distress or violence, they even went
about their flagellation with an appearance
of pleasure, or at least of nonchalance, so
marked that they might have been chatter-
ing about other matters, laughing, bawling
about the street, running and leaping when
there was so great a crowd that the procession
fell somewhat into confusion. Along with
them went certain men carrying wine, which
was offered to them now and again, and
some of them took a mouthful thereof, and
sometimes sweetmeats were given. The wine-

---

[1] *Essais*, i. 11. "Mais ne veoid on encores touts les
jours, au vendredi sainct, en divers lieux, un grand
nombre d'hommes et de femmes se battre jusques à se
deschirer la chair et percer jusques aux os? Cela ay je
veu souvent et sans enchantement : et disoit on (car ils
vont masquez) qu'il y en avoit qui pour de l'argent entre-
prenoient en cela de garantir la religion d'aultruy, par
un mépris de la douleur d'autant plus grand, que plus
peuvent les aiguillons de la dévotion que de l'avarice."

carriers often took wine in their mouths and
then blew it out and moistened therewith the
lashes of the scourges, which were of cord,
and were wont to become coagulated with
the blood drawn to such an extent that it
was necessary to moisten them in order to
separate the thongs. They also blew the
wine over the wounds of some of the vic-
tims. The appearance of their shoes and
breeches suggested that they were people of
mean condition, and that the majority of
them had sold themselves to this service.
Moreover, I was told that they were wont to
grease their shoulders with a certain preparation, but the wounds I saw were so
natural, and the scourging was so lengthy,
that assuredly no medicament could benumb
them to pain. And with regard to those
who may have hired them, what profit
would they get were this exhibition nought
but trickery ? Certain other peculiarities of
this function may be noticed. When the
people in procession arrive at Saint Peter's the
only function they attend is the exhibition

of *il Viso Santo*, and as soon as one company has seen it, it passes on and makes room for another. On this day great liberty is granted to all womankind; for, through the night, the streets are filled with ladies nearly all going on foot. Nevertheless the city has the air of having greatly mended its manners, especially in respect to the relaxation aforesaid, all amorous glances and manifestations being suppressed.

The church of Santa Rotonda makes the fairest show at this season on account of its illumination. Amongst other devices a vast number of lamps, hung from the top to the bottom of the church, are kept in constant motion. On Easter eve I saw at Saint John Lateran the heads of Saint Paul and Saint Peter, which have still some flesh upon them, and are coloured and bearded as in life.[1] The face of Saint Peter is fair, somewhat elongated, with a ruddy, almost sanguine

[1] An account of these relics may be found in Cancellieri, *Memorie istoriche delle sagre teste dei SS. Apostoli P. e P.* (Roma, 1806), and in the Dictionary of Moroni, *Teste dei SS. Pietro e Paolo.*

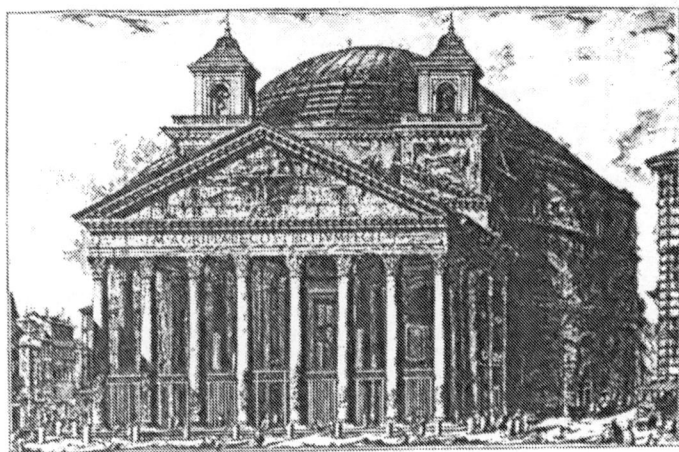

THE PANTHEON

tint on the cheeks, and a forked grey beard, the head being covered with a papal mitre. That of Saint Paul is dark, broad, and fatter; the head altogether being larger and the beard thick and grey. They are kept high up in a place devised for them, and the exhibition is made in this wise. The people are summoned by the ringing of bells, then a curtain, stretched before the heads, is let down, and they may be seen side by side. They are left visible long enough to let the spectators say an *Ave Maria*, and then the curtain is drawn up again. Afterwards they are displayed afresh in the same way, and then for a third time. This exhibition takes place three or four times during the day. The place where they are kept is about the height of a pike from the ground, and a heavy iron grating is in front of them, through which the spectator must peer in order to see them, several candles being lighted outside the grating, but it is difficult to discern clearly the particular features. I saw them three or four times, and found the skin shiny and something like the masks we use.

On the Wednesday after Easter M. Maldonat,[1] who was then at Rome, inquired of me what might be my opinion of the ways and habits of the city, especially with respect to religion. It happened that our views agreed exactly, to wit, that the common people were beyond comparison more devout in France than in Rome, while the contrary might be affirmed of the richer classes, and especially of those about the court. He told me that whenever he heard men maintain that France was altogether given over to heresy—and especially when the disputants were Spaniards, of whom there were great number in his society—he always answered that more truly religious men might be found in Paris alone than in the whole of Spain.

In bringing boats up the Tiber they tow them with three or four pairs of buffaloes. I know not how others find the air of Rome, but I myself found it very pleasant and

[1] Montaigne met Maldonat at Epernay, vol. i., p. 32.

healthy. The Sieur de Vielart told me that since he had been there he had lost all tendency to headache, an observation which goes to confirm that held by the Romans themselves : that the air is bad for the feet, but good for the head. Nothing is so adverse to my own health as listlessness and sloth, and in Rome I was never without occupation, which, though it may not have been always so pleasant as I could have wished, yet served to keep me from tedium. For instance, I visited and inspected the antiquities and the vineyards, which here are gardens and pleasure places of extraordinary beauty. There I learned how susceptible to the touch of art were these rough, rocky, and unlevel spots of ground, for the artificers here have contrived to win from them a graceful effect, impossible to imitate in our level country, and to turn these irregularities to advantage with the utmost skill. Amongst the most beautiful of these gardens are those of the Cardinals d'Este at Monte Cavallo, and Farnese at the Palatine ; of

Cardinals Orsini, Sforza, and Medici; of
Papa Giulio and of Madama; those of the
Farnese and of Cardinal Riario in Trastevere,
and of Cesio outside the Porta del Popolo.[1]
All these beautiful spots are free and open
to any one who may desire to enter therein,
or even to pass the night there with some
chosen companion whenever the owners
chance to be away, and they are scarcely
ever in residence.　Then there are always
sermons to be listened to at all seasons, or
disputes in theology; or again diversion
may be found with some courtesan or other,
but in this case I found one disadvantage, to
wit, that these ladies charge as extortionately
for the privilege of simple conversation (which
was what I sought, desiring to hear them
talk, and to take part in their play of wit) as

[1] Of these gardens the Villa d'Este is now covered by
the palace and gardens of the Quirinale. The Orsini
possessed gardens or vineyards on Monte Cavallo, on
the Pincio, and on the Aventine. The Sforza had one
garden near Monte Testaccio and one near the Bar-
berini Palace. The Farnese, Medici, Madama, and Papa
Giulio exist at present. The Farnese *a Trastevere* is
now the site of the Villa Farnesina.

for the supreme favour, and are just as niggard thereof. All these recreations kept me free effectually from melancholy, which is the death of me, and of irritability, with which I was troubled neither without doors nor within. Thus I found Rome a very pleasant place of sojourn, and I might go on to show that, if I had penetrated more deeply into the inner life of the place, I might have been still more pleased; for I must admit that, though I used all possible care and ingenuity, I only gathered acquaintance with the public aspect of the city, the same that she shows to the meanest stranger.

On Low Sunday I witnessed the ceremony of the bestowal of alms on certain young maidens. On this day the Pope had, in addition to his ordinary equipage, twenty-five horses led before him, decked and covered with cloth of gold, and most richly caparisoned, and ten or twelve mules covered with crimson velvet, all these being led by his lackeys on foot. Then came the Pope's litter, also covered with crimson velvet. The

Pope himself rode on his mule, and before him went four men on horseback who carried each one a cardinal's hat, set on the top of a staff which was covered with red velvet and gilt about the handle and the top. The cardinals who followed rode also on mules and wore their pontifical garb, the skirts of their robes being fastened by pins to the mules' bridles. The maidens numbered a hundred and seven, each one being accompanied by an elderly kinswoman, and when the mass was finished they left the church and marched in a long procession. Having re-entered the church of La Minerva—where this function takes place—they passed one by one through the choir and kissed the feet of the Pope; who, after blessing them, gave them each from his own hand a purse of white damask containing a note on his bankers. It was understood that all these girls have found husbands, wherefore they come to ask for a dowry, which is fixed at a sum of thirty-five crowns apiece, in addition to the white robe costing five crowns, which they wear at their wedding. Their faces were covered with linen veils, with no opening save holes to look through.[1]

I was speaking lately of the advantages of Rome, and will now add, in reference to this matter, that I find it, of all towns in the world, the one most filled with the corporate idea, in which difference of nationality counts least; for, by its very nature, it is a patchwork of strangers, each one being as much at home as in his own country. The authority of its ruler lies over the whole of Christianity.[2] By his own will he, as the

---

[1] This function was the charge of the Confraternity of the Annunziata, founded in 1460, and attached to the church of S. Maria sopra Minerva by Pius II. Pius V. and Urban VII. left thereto large benefactions.

[2] *Essais*, iii. 9: " Et puis cette mesme Rome que nous voyons, merite qu'on l'aime : confederée de si longtemps, et par tant de tiltres à nostre Couronne : seule ville commune et universelle. Le Magistrat souverain qui y commande, est recognu pareillement ailleurs : c'est la ville Métropolitaine de toutes les nations Chrestiennes. L'Espagnol et le François chacun y est chez soy : pour estre des princes de cet Estat, il ne faut estre que de Chrestienté où qu'elle soit. Il n'est lieu ça bas que le Ciel ait embrassé avec telle influence de faveur et telle constance : sa ruine mesme est glorieuse et enflée."

supreme arbiter of right and wrong, can compel the obedience of strangers in their own lands, just the same as if they were denizens of Rome. Considerations of birth have no weight in the promotion of men to high office in his court. The freedom given under the government of Venice, and the conveniences of traffic, attract thither vast numbers of foreigners, but they are nevertheless like men in a stranger city; while here foreigners will be found in special offices carrying emolument and responsibility, for Rome is the home of all those connected with the Church. As many or perhaps more strangers may be seen in Venice (where the multitude of these far exceeds anything of the sort in France or Germany), but not nearly so many resident or domiciled foreigners. The common people are no longer affronted by the sight of a man dressed in French, or Spanish, or German fashion, and nearly every beggar who begged alms of me spoke my own tongue.

However, I sought in every way and

used all my five natural senses to win for myself the title of Roman citizen, if only for the ancient renown and religious association clinging to the position attached to this citizenship. I found the task a difficult one, nevertheless I accomplished it without having availed myself of any man's favour, or indeed letting the matter come to the knowledge of any Frenchman. I enlisted the Pope's interest, which was brought to bear by Filippo Murotti, the major-domo, who had always been extraordinarily kind to me, and had taken special trouble in this particular affair.[1] Certain letters, bearing the date 3° *Id. Martii* 1581, and relating to the business, were sent off and reached me on April 5th. They were in full official style, in the same form and friendly expression as those sent to the Seigneur Giacomo Buoncompagno, Duke of Sora, the Pope's son. This title is now altogether a vain one, nevertheless I felt

[1] Montaigne writes at length over this event in *Essais*, iii. 9.

much pleasure from the possession of the same.

On April 3rd I left Rome early in the morning by the Porta San Lorenzo, *Tiburtina*. The road I took was fairly level, and ran through a country which was for the most part fertile cornland and sparsely populated, like all the approaches to Rome. I crossed the Teverone, anciently the Anio, first at the bridge of Mammolo, and second by that of Lucan, the old name of this bridge being still retained. On this bridge are divers ancient inscriptions, and the chief of these is still easily legible; moreover, two or three Roman tombs are yet standing along this road. Few other antiquities are to be seen, and on the *Via Tiburtina* itself only a very little of the ancient pavement in great blocks. After a journey of fifteen miles, I arrived in time for dinner at Tivoli, the ancient Tiburtum.

This town lies at the foot of a range of mountains, the houses being built along the somewhat steep ascent of the lower slopes.

TIVOLI

From Civitates Orbis Terrarum

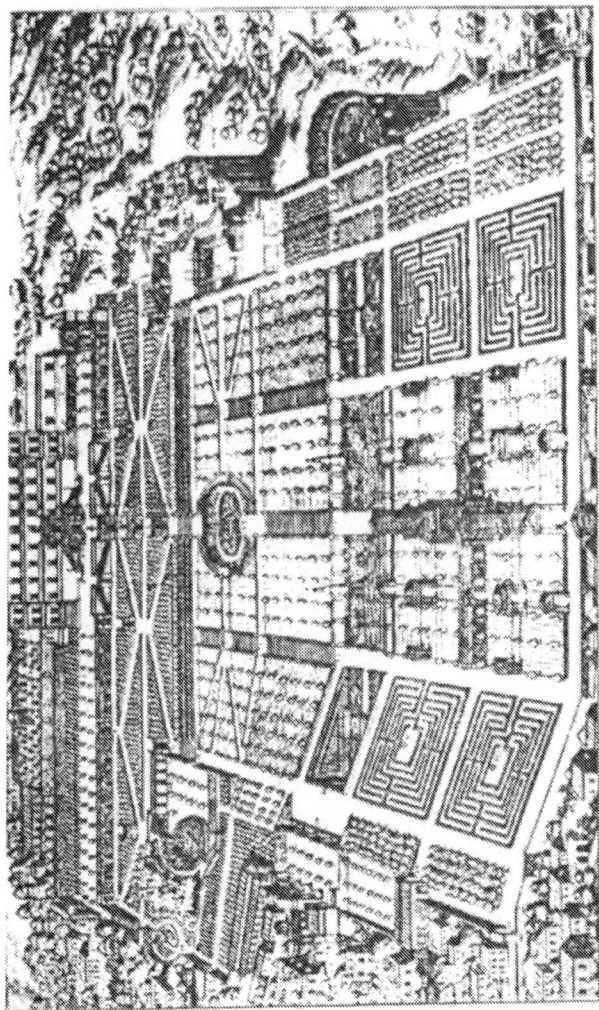

On this account the site and the prospect therefrom are magnificent, forasmuch as the view extends over a boundless plain, and includes the great city of Rome. It faces the sea, the mountains stand in the rear, the stream of the Teverone flows through it and, close by, takes a marvellous leap, descending from the mountains and disappearing in a chasm of the rocks some five or six hundred paces below. Afterwards it reaches the plain, where it follows a course greatly varied, and joins the Tiber a little above the city. In Tivoli is to be seen the famous palace and garden of the cardinal of Ferrara, a most exquisite piece of work, but unfinished in several parts and likely to remain so, as the cardinal now owning it has stopped all operations.[1] I looked at everything minutely, and I would attempt to set down here some representation thereof, if so many books and illustrations had not been already

[1] The Villa d'Este was built by Pirro Ligorio for the Cardinal Ippolito d'Este, son of Alfonso II. of Ferrara, in the middle of the sixteenth century. Eustace, who visited it in 1801, describes it as fallen to decay.

published.		This outburst of a countless
number of jets of water, turned on or off
by a single appliance manipulated at some
distant point, I had seen elsewhere during
my travels, notably at Florence and Augs-
burg, as I have already recorded.		Here
real music is produced from a sort of natural
organ, which always plays the same tune, by
the means of water which falls with great
force into a round vaulted recess where it
disturbs the air and forces it to seek an exit,
and at the same time supplies the wind
necessary to make the organ pipes sound.
Another stream of water turns a wheel
fitted with teeth, which are set so as to strike
in a certain order the keyboard of the organ,
and the sound of trumpets is also counter-
feited by the same agency.

In another place one may hear the song of
birds, which is produced by small bronze
flutes, such as are seen at feasts, and give
a sound similar to that produced from those
little earthen vessels full of water into which
children blow with a mouthpiece.		This is

worked by mechanism like that used in the organs; and by another device an owl is made to appear on the top of a rock, whereupon all the harmony ceases at once, the birds being terrified at his presence. Then the owl retires and they sing again. Thus they may be brought forward and made to retire in turn as long as any one likes. Elsewhere a noise like the report of a cannon is produced, and again other sounds, less loud and very frequent, like the fusilade of arquebusiers. This is made by the sudden falling of water into certain pipes, the air therein, by struggling to find a vent, causing this noise. These same inventions, or something like to them, working by the same natural causes, I have seen in other places.

There are many pools or reservoirs edged all round with stone balustrades, on the top of which are set divers high columns of stone, distant one from the other about four paces. From the summits of these pillars the water spouts forth with strong impetus, not upward, but down towards the water in the basin.   All the jets, being turned inwards and facing one another, discharge the water into the tank with such velocity that, when the threads of water collide in the air, they let descend into the basin a thick and continual mist.   The sun falling upon the same produces on the surface of the basin, in the air, and all round about, a rainbow so marked and so like nature that it in no way falls short of the bow seen in the sky.   I saw nought to equal this elsewhere.

Under the palace itself are several vast cellars and ventilating chambers, artificially made, which give out a cooling vapour and temper the air in the basement, but this portion of the palace is still imperfect.   In this villa I observed many statues of great merit, the most notable being two nymphs, one dead, and the other asleep; a Pallas with divine attributes; a replica of the Adonis which is in the palace of the bishop of Aquino; a wolf in bronze; a boy extracting a thorn, like the one in the Capitol; the Laocoon and the Antinous, after those

in the Belvedere; the Comedy, also of
the Capitol; and the Satyr of the country
villa of Cardinal Sforza; a copy of a recent
work, the Moses, from the tomb in S. Pietro
in Vinculo, and of the beautiful woman who
is at the feet of Pope Paul III. in the new
church of Saint Peter's.   These same statues,
indeed, gave me greater pleasure than any
others in Rome.[1]

Pratolino was certainly built in rivalry
with this place.   In the richness and beauty
of the grottoes Florence is far superior, but
the gardens of the cardinal of Ferrara sur-
pass Pratolino in abundance of water.   As
to the various diverting artifices produced by
water-work, they are about the same, what
though the Florentine designer may have
produced a more elegant effect in laying out

---

[1] The statues which Montaigne saw were all found in
Hadrian's Villa.   In 1780 a certain number of them were
taken by Duke Ercole III. to Modena, and the re-
mainder removed to Rome and added to the Capitoline
Museum.   The last-named statue was covered with a
bronze robe by Bernini in deference to current notions of
propriety.

and ordering the ground. This palace certainly has the advantage in antique statues,
and in the house itself. The Florentine
erection, in the beauty of its site, and in the
view over the adjacent country, is vastly
superior to that of the cardinal of Ferrara.
I should, however, have nothing but praise
for the natural surroundings of the villa at
Tivoli were it not that by ill-luck all the
water therein, except that flowing from a
fountain in a little garden high up, of some
which is brought into one of the apartments
of the palace itself, is the water of the
Teverone, a branch of which the cardinal
has manipulated and cut therefor a special
canal for his own use. If this water were
only clear and good to drink, instead of being
turbulent and dirty, this place would stand
beyond all comparison, especially with regard
to the great fountain and its adjuncts, which
in construction and aspect is the most exquisite work to be seen in this garden or in
any other place. At Pratolino, on the other
hand, all the water comes from springs, and

is brought from afar.   For the reason that
the Teverone comes down from mountains
still higher than those of Tivoli, divers of
the people of the neighbourhood make
what use they list of the river water,
wherefore the cardinal's handiwork seems
less noteworthy, because others have done
the same thing.

On the morrow I departed after dinner,
and passed by a vast ruin on the right-hand
side of the road, which is by report six miles
in extent.   This was formerly a villa, and
known as the *prædium* of the Emperor
Adrian.[1]   The road from Tivoli to Rome
crosses a rivulet impregnated with sulphur.
The banks of the stream are all white therewith, and the stench may be smelt half a
league away, but no medicinal use is made of
the water.   In this stream may be found
divers little substances compounded of the
scum of the water, which are so much like
our medicinal powder that few could tell the

[1] This is all the mention he makes of Hadrian's
Villa.

difference, and the people of Tivoli make
out of this same material all sorts of medica-
ments, two boxes of which I bought for
seven sous and six deniers. In Tivoli are
divers antiquities, two terminal images of
a very ancient shape, and the remains of a
temple with several columns still perfect,
which legend declares to have been the
temple of the ancient Sibyl. However, on
the cornice thereof there may still be seen
five or six large letters; but this inscription
seems to have been left unfinished, for the
stonework beyond them is still intact.
Whether any other letters preceded these
I know not, as on that side the wall is
ruined. All that are now visible run as follows: Ce . . . Ellius L. F. What may be
their signification I cannot say.

In the evening we arrived at Rome after
a journey of fifteen miles. I travelled in a
coach without any tedium or discomfort, a
rare experience with me. The people here
pay more careful heed to one particular
usage than in any other place; that is to say,

THE TEMPLE OF THE SIBYL AT TIVOLI

for the sake of health they find out the different characteristics of the various streets and quarters of the city, and even of the suites of apartments in their houses. This consideration is held to be of such high importance that they always change their residence according to the seasons. Even those who live in hired dwellings maintain at great cost three or four houses, so that they may shift at the proper season according to the advice of their physicians.

On the 15th of April I went to take leave of the Maestro del Sacro Palazzo[1] and his associate. They begged me "to pay no regard to the censures which had been passed upon my book; censures which, as certain Frenchmen had informed them, contained many ignorant statements: they declared that they honoured my purpose, my affection towards the Church, and my ability: that they rated my good breeding and conscientiousness highly enough to allow

[1] Montaigne notes his first interview with this official and the objections taken to his writings on page 139.

me at my own discretion to cut out of my
book with my own hand, at the next re-
printing of the same, any passages which
might seem too plain spoken, and amongst
others those remarks about Fortune." 'It
seemed to me that they were not ill pleased
with me: moreover, to justify their careful
examination of my book and their con-
demnation of the same in divers particulars,
they instanced several contemporary books,
written by cardinals and ecclesiastical personages of high repute, which had been
censured for blots of a like character, the
good name of the author and the book itself
having been left quite scatheless thereby.
They ended by begging me to give the
Church the benefit of my eloquence (these
are their usual *mots de courtoisie*) and to make
my abode with them in this peaceful and
untroubled city. Both of these men were
of high authority and competent for the
cardinalate.

We tasted artichokes, beans, and peas about
the middle of March.

In April it is light at what they call ten hours,[1] and, as I well believe, at nine when the days are at their longest.

It was at this time that I made the acquaintance of a certain Pole, who had been the most intimate friend of Cardinal Hosius.[2] This man presented to me two copies of a book which he had written with great care concerning the cardinal's death.   The pleasure of a sojourn in this city becomes vastly greater by usage.   I never breathed air more pleasant or more·healthy to my temperament.

On the 18th of April I went to view the

[1] 4 A.M.

[2] Stanislaus Hosius or Hozyusz was a native of Cracow, and was educated at Padua, where he was a fellow-student with Reginald Pole, and at Bologna.   He introduced the Jesuits into Poland in 1569, and was charged with many confidential missions between Pius IV. and the Emperor Ferdinand during the sittings of the Council of Trent. He founded the hospital of S. Stanislaus for his countrymen in Rome.   He died at Capranica in 1579. Possibly the Pole mentioned by Montaigne was Stanislaus Reskke, who has left a life of Cardinal Hosius, *Stanislai Hosii Cardinalis Vita*, Roma, 1587.

inside of the palace of Signor Giov. Giorgio
Cesarini, which contains countless rare antiquities, the most noteworthy of which are the
authentic busts of Zeno, Possidonius, Euri-
pides, and Carneades, according to the very
ancient Greek inscriptions which are thereon.
I saw also portraits of the fairest Roman
ladies of the present day and of the owner's
wife, the Signora Clælia Fascia Farnese, who,
though she may not be the most beautiful,
is assuredly the most amiable lady in Rome;
or, for all I know, in the whole world.[1]
This nobleman boasts descent from the race
of the Cæsars, and by this right carries the
banner of the Roman nobility.   He is a rich
man, and he bears for arms the column with

---

[1] She was the daughter of Cardinal Alessandro Farnese,
who, according to the current saying in Rome, had made
the three most beautiful things in the city : the Palazzo
Farnese, the Church of the Gesù, and La bella Clelia.
After the death of her husband in 1585, she gave occasion for scandal on account of her connection with the
Cardinal dei Medici and Alfonso Vitelli.   Her father
ultimately compelled her to marry Marco Pio of Savoy,
who was ten years her junior.   The marriage was an
unhappy one.

PALAZZO FARNESE

the bear attached thereto, and above the column an eagle with outspread wings. The vineyards are amongst the most beautiful features of Rome, and these are in season in midsummer.

VIII

ROME TO LORETO

On Wednesday, April 19th, I quitted
Rome after dinner, being escorted as far
as the Ponte Molle by Messieurs de Mar-
montier,[1] De la Trimouille, Du Bellay, and
divers other gentlemen.   When we had
crossed the bridge we turned to the right,
leaving to our left the high-road to Viterbo
by which we had entered Rome, and having
on our right the Tiber and the mountains.
We followed a road, exposed and very uneven, running through a barren country void
of inhabitants, and passed the spot known
as the *Prima porta*, *i.e.* the first gate, situated seven miles from Rome.   Some hold
that the ancient walls of Rome reached to
this point, but I cannot see how this can

---

[1] Probably a misprint for Noirmôutier.

be true. Along this road, which is the
ancient Via Flaminia, are situated divers rare
antiquities about which nought is known.
After riding sixteen miles, we arrived at bedtime at Castel Nuovo.

This is a small village belonging to the
Colonnas, lying buried amongst the low
hills, in a situation which strongly reminded
me of the fertile passes in our Pyrenees on
the road to Aigues Caudes. On the next
day, April 20th, we went on through the
same sort of country, mountainous but very
pleasing, fertile, and well peopled, till we
arrived at a gorge beside the Tiber in which
was situated Borghetto, a small village belonging to Duke Ottavio Farnese. We
resumed our journey when we had dined,
and, after traversing an exceedingly pleasant
valley with low hills on either side, we
crossed the Tiber at Corde,[1] where may still
be seen vast piles of stone, the ruins of the

---

[1] Orte. The foundations of the present bridge are the
work of Augustus ; the more recent portions having been
built by Sixtus V.

bridge which Augustus caused to be built
in order that the country of the Sabines,
towards which we were travelling, might
be united to that of the Faliscii on the
other side of the river. We next came to
Otricoli, a small village belonging to the
cardinal of Perugia,[1] in front of which, in
a very fine situation, are some large and
important ruins. The country, mountainous
and exceedingly pleasant of aspect, is everywhere broken and uneven, but very fertile
and populous. On this road we passed an
inscription which proclaimed how the Pope
had made and levelled this road, which he
called *Viam Boncompagnam* after his own
name. This custom, a common one in
Italy and Germany, of thus setting up a
written record as a testimony of works of
this sort, is an excellent stimulus to urge
on men of that temper which recks little
of the public weal to execute some useful
work, from the hope of gaining fame and

---

[1] He had invited Montaigne to dine with him at his
villa near Porto. See page 128.

reputation thereby. In sooth this road was formerly, for the most part of the way, uncomfortable to travel, whereas now it has been made level enough for coaches as far as Loreto. After travelling ten miles we arrived in time for bed at Narni, which in Latin is called *Narnia*.

This little town belongs to the Church. It stands on the top of a rock at the base of which flows the river Negra, or in Latin *Nar*, one side of the town being situated so as to overlook a pleasant plain through which the river goes joyously along and winds in marvellous fashion. In the public place is a very fine fountain. I went to see the cathedral, and remarked that the tapestry therein bears divers inscriptions and rhymes written in our old French tongue. I was not able to ascertain whence it came, although I learned from the people of the place that they had always been well disposed towards our nation. This tapestry shows forth the story of the Passion and occupies one entire side of the nave. For

the reason that Pliny declares that in this
country is found a certain sort of earth
which softens with the heat and dries up
in the rain, I made inquiries of the inhabitants concerning the same, but they
could tell me nought thereof. About a
mile distant there are some springs of cold
water which work the same effects as our
hot ones. Certain patients still make trial
of them, but they are in no great repute.
The inn, judged by the Italian standard,
was a good one. We had no candles, all
the house being lighted by oil.

Early on the morning of the 21st, we
went down the very pleasant valley along
which runs the Negra. This stream we
crossed by a bridge at the very gates of
Terni,[1] where in the public place, we remarked a very ancient column still upright.
I found no inscription thereon, but at the
side is an effigy of a lion in relief, below

[1] It is strange that Montaigne, with his partiality for
artificial waterworks, should leave the Falls of Terni
unnoticed.

which is a dedication to Neptune in ancient
characters, and also Neptune himself sculptured in marble with his customary train.[1]
In this same place is an inscription in a
prominent position in honour of a certain
A. Pompeius A. F. The people of the
town, which was known as *Interamnia*, because of the river Negra which passes close
on one side and of a brook which flows on

---

[1] L'Angeloni, in his *Storia di Terni* (Pisa, 1878),
describes a figure of Neptune found in some excavations
near Lago Velino with the following inscription :—

Neptuno Sacrum
L. Valerius Nigri Lib. Menander
Portitor Ocrisiva.

He also gives the inscription mentioned by Montaigne:—

A. Pompejo A. F.
Clu. Q. Patrono
Municipi Interamnat.
Nahartis quod ejus
Opera universum
Municipium ex summis
Periculis et Diffi-
cultatibus expeditum
et conservatum est ex
Testamento L. Licini T. F.
Statua statuta est.

the other, erected a statue to this man in
memory of the services which he had
wrought, but it is no longer to be seen.
I calculated the antiquity of the inscription
aforesaid by the use made of diphthongs in
writing *periculeis* and other similar words.
The town occupies a very pleasant site. At
the bottom of the valley, by the road we
had traversed, the level ground is very
fertile, and farther on the sides of the hills
are populous and well tilled, the abundance
of olive trees making a picture as fair as
the eye could wish, while here and there
along these slopes arise tall mountains, which
display themselves well cultivated and productive of all manner of fruits up to the
very tops. For the last four-and-twenty
hours I had been grievously tormented with
colic, and at this moment the pain was at
its worst, but I did not on this account fail
to enjoy the beauty of the country around
me.

After our departure we found ourselves
in the passes of the Apennines, and then we

were able to appreciate what a great and seemly and noble work the Pope has accomplished in the making of this new road at such a vast expense and labour. The neighbouring people were forced to give their labour in its formation, and they do not complain on this account so much as of the fact that all the land required for the road, whether arable, orchard, or aught else, was taken from them and no price paid therefor. On our right hand we perceived a little town placed on the summit of a pleasant elevation, called Colle Scipoli, or, according to ancient usage, *Castrum Scipionis*. The other mountains are lofty, arid, and rocky; and faring between these and what must be in winter the channel of a torrent, we arrived at Spoleto after travelling eighteen miles.

This is a famous and well-built city, situated in a hollow amongst the mountains. There we were compelled to show our *bolletta*, not by reason of the plague, of which all Italy was then free, but on account of a

certain Petrino,[1] a citizen of the place, and
the most notorious bandit of the country, of
whom wonderful stories are told. The people
of Spoleto and of all the towns round about
were in great fear that they should be taken
unawares by him. This country is thick set
with taverns, even in places where there are
no houses. These they make out of the
boughs of trees, where you will find tables
spread with boiled eggs and cheese and wine.
They have no butter, but serve everything
fried in oil.

On leaving the town this same day after

---

[1] Petrino was one of the most celebrated brigands of
the cinquecento. He began his career about 1577, and
for several years afterwards kept in terror the duchy of
Spoleto and the south of Umbria. He was active in these
parts as late as 1581. His death and capture were several
times reported, but he seems to have escaped to Spain,
where he lived until 1640, and returned under the favour of
the Farnesi. He died at an advanced age in 1650.

Brigandage was rife throughout the papal territories at
this time. Gregory XIII. was on bad terms with all his
neighbours on account of his arrogance and extortions,
and the Florentines and Venetians allowed the bandits
to take refuge in their dominions when pressed by the
papal forces. It is strange that Montaigne should have
had so little to say about it.

dinner, we found ourselves in the valley of
Spoleto, a plain lying between the mountains,
and as fair a one as the fancy can picture,
and two good Gascon leagues in width. We
could likewise discern many houses on the
crests of the adjacent hills. The road running
through this plain is a continuation of the
papal road I have just spoken of, being made
like a high-road as straight as a line; and in
our course we passed many towns on either
hand—amongst others, on the right, was
Trevi. Servius, in his comment on Virgil,
declares that this is the place to which the
poet refers in Book VII. as *oliviferæque
Mutiscæ*, a view which certain other writers
contradict. However this may be, it is a
town built on the side of a high hill, occupying
a site which reaches half-way up the slope,
and most pleasantly situated, the mountain
being covered throughout with olive trees.
Pursuing this road, which was renovated three
years ago and is now the finest that can anywhere be seen, we arrived in the evening at
Foligno, after travelling twelve miles.

This is a fair town situated on a plain,
which, as I neared it, reminded me strongly
of the plain of St. Foi,[1] though it was beyond all comparison richer and the town
more seemly and populous. It is situated
on a rivulet called the Topino, and was
formerly known as Fulignium or Fulcinia,
being built on the site of the Forum Flam-
inium. On this road the inns are for the
most part as good as those of France, except
that they hardly ever provide other food than
hay for the horses, and salt fish is almost
always served in lieu of fresh. Moreover,
all through Italy they eat beans raw, and
peas and almonds green, and rarely cook
their artichokes. The floors are paved with
tiles. They hold in their oxen by the nose,
by means of a piece of iron which pierces the
division of the nostrils, the same as that used
for buffaloes. Their baggage mules, which
are excellent and very plentiful, are not shod
before in our fashion, but with a round shoe,

[1] Sainte Foix, in Périgord, close to Montaigne's
home.

which is larger than the foot and goes all round it. At divers spots there are monks whose wont it is to give holy water to travellers, and to look for an alms in return; and crowds of children who beg for money, and promise to say a dozen paternosters on the beads which they hold in their hands in return for what may be given to them. The wines are poor.

On the morning of the morrow, after quitting this beautiful plain, we once more set out along the mountain road, on which we encountered many fine level spaces, some on high ground and some on low. In the early part of the morning we enjoyed for a time a most exquisite view of a thousand varied hills, clad everywhere with the finest shady trees or by fruit trees of all sorts, or by the richest corn-fields, the ground being often so steep and broken that it seemed a marvel how horses could find their way thither. These lovely valleys, the countless brooks, and the houses and villages on every side, reminded one of the roads near Florence, except that here are no palaces or houses of consequence, and round Florence the land is arid and barren for the most part, unlike these hills where scarce a span of vacant ground is to be seen. Certes, I saw it at its best in the spring-time. Often we could espy one village far up over our heads and another beneath our feet, each well fitted with the conveniences of life. What made the prospect all the more delightful was that, beyond these fertile hills, we could distinguish the rugged and inaccessible summits of the Apennines, and the torrents descending therefrom, which, when they have lost their primal impulse, come down into the valleys as gracious and gentle brooks. While traversing these hills we could see, both on the heights and down below, many fertile level fields, some of them wider than the eye could cover on account of a slight slope in the distance, the landscape being of a beauty and richness beyond the power of a painter to imitate. Onward hence the aspect of our road took a varied character, but the highway was always easy and level; and, after a twenty-mile journey, we came, in time for dinner, to La Maccia, a little town on the river Chiento.

We kept along the road, which took an easy course at the base of the mountains, and here I had a dispute with the *vetturino* and gave him a box on the ear, which the custom of this country rates as a violent outrage; as is exemplified by the case of the *vetturino* who, for a similar assault, killed the Prince of Tresignano. As I saw that the fellow had left our company, and felt some apprehension lest he should make a charge against me or work other mischief, I changed my plan, which was to push on to Tolentino, and halted for supper at Val Chimara, a small village at the end of the eighth mile, situated on the bank of the Chiento. On the morrow, Sunday, we kept along the valley between fertile and cultivated mountain slopes, as far as the little town of Tolentino, through which we passed, and then came to a more level region. Now on either side the hills were small and easy of access, the whole region reminding me strongly of L'Agenois [1] in the fairest part thereof beside the Garonne, except that here, as in Switzerland, no castles or gentlemen's houses are to be seen, but many villages and towns are built on the hill sides.   We made our journey along the Chiento over a very fine road, the latter part of which was paved with brick, for twenty-eight miles, and reached Macerata for dinner.

This is a fine town, about the size of Libourne, built in circular form on a hill, and rising equally on all sides towards its centre. It contains very few houses of consequence, but I remarked one palace of hewn stone enriched outside with square diamonds rising to a point like the palace of the Cardinal d'Este at Ferrara,[2] a design which gives a very pleasing appearance. At the entrance of

---

[1] Now the department of Lot-et-Garonne.   Matteo Bandello had held the bishopric of Agen until a few years before this time.

[2] The Palazzo dei Diamanti, now the Pinacoteca, built for Sigismondo d'Este in 1493.   The building alluded to by Montaigne is probably the Palazzo Mignardi.

this town is a new gate with the inscription,
Porta Boncompaigno, written in letters of gold,
which gate stands on one of the roads which
the reigning Pope has reinstated. The town
is the residence of the legate for the Marches.
On these routes they serve the travellers
with wine that has been boiled, their custom
being to boil it until it shall have shrunk one-
half, in order to improve it. By this time
we were advised by the crowds of people
going and coming that we were on the road
to Loreto. Besides many single pilgrims,
were troops of rich people going on foot in
pilgrim garb, some of these companies being
distinguished by a flag and by a crucifix, which
was carried in front, and by a particular sort
of dress. After dinner we traversed an un-
interesting country, now passing over plains
and small rivers and now over gentle hills,
but all the way the land was very fertile and
the road for the most part paved with tiles
set on edge. We passed through Recanati,
a straggling town on high ground, which
adapts itself to the hills and hollows of its

site, and arrived in the evening at Loreto, having gone fifteen miles.

Loreto is a small village enclosed with walls and fortified against attack by the Turks,[1] and built on a slightly elevated plain. It overlooks a very fair stretch of country, and is not far from the shores of the Adriatic Sea or Gulf of Venice; indeed they say that in fine weather the Sclavonic mountains on the other side may be seen. The town contains few inhabitants except those who serve the needs of the religious devotees, some as innkeepers—and their lodgings are dirty enough—and some as traffickers, that is, vendors of tapers, images, paternosters, Agnus Dei, Saviours, and wares of this sort, many of these dealers having fine and well-furnished shops, in which I, personally, left behind some fifty good crowns. The priests and church officials and the College of Jesuits are all lodged together in a large modern palace, where lives also the governor, a cleric,

[1] In the time of Leo X. the neighbouring city of Recanati had been burnt by the Turks.

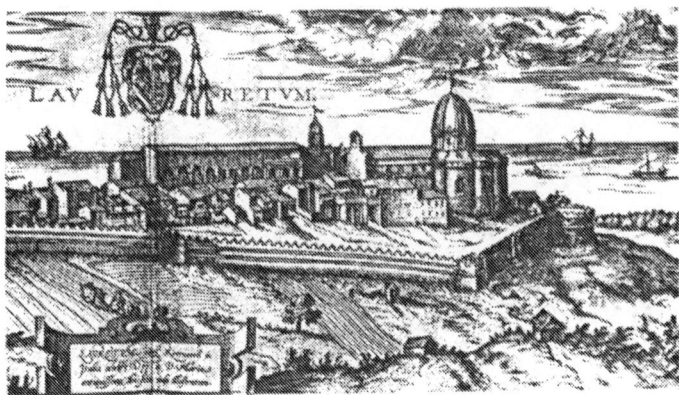

LORETO

From Civitates Orbis Terrarum

To face p. 236, vol. ii.

to whom, as representative of the legate and the Pope, all applications must be addressed.

The holy place is a little house, very old and mean, built of brick,[1] and much greater in length than in width. At the upper end thereof a barrier has been constructed, having on either side a gate of iron, and between these an iron grating, the whole fabric being rude and old and lacking in all richness of furniture. The iron grating aforesaid fills up the space between the two doors, and through it the spectator can see to the end of the recess, and the extreme end, the shrine, occupies about a fifth part of the space thus enclosed. This is the spot of the highest sanctity. There may be seen on the upper part of the wall the image of Our Lady, made, so the story goes, of wood. All the residue of the shrine is so thickly covered with rich *ex votos* given by divers cities and princes that, right down to the

[1] The Santa Casa is built of stone and not of brick.

ground, there is not an inch of space which is not covered with some device of gold or silver. With great difficulty and as a high favour done to me, I was able to find a place whereon I could fix a memorial device, in which were set four silver figures, that of Our Lady, my own, my wife's, and my daughter's. On the base of mine was engraved on the silver the inscription, "Michael Montanus Gallus Vasco, Eques Regii Ordinis, 1581." On my wife's, "Francisca Cassaniana, uxor," and on my daughter's, "Leonora Montana, filia unica." These three are all kneeling in a row before Our Lady, who is set somewhat higher. The chapel has another entrance besides the two of which I have spoken, and any one entering it thereby will find my tablet on the left-hand side, opposite the door in the corner, the same having been very carefully fixed and nailed to the wall. I had caused a chain and ring of silver to be fitted thereto, so as to let it hang from a nail, but the chapel officials preferred to fasten it to the wall

itself.[1]   In this small enclosure is the fireplace
of the cottage, and this they exhibit by draw-
ing aside some ancient tapestries which hang
before it.   Very few persons are allowed to
enter here, indeed there is a notice over the
door forbidding admission to any one not
furnished with the leave of the governor.
These doors are of metal, very richly worked,
and an iron grating is fixed in front of them.

Amongst the other rich and rare offerings
left there I saw a candle recently sent by a
Turk who had made a vow to Our Lady
when he was in sore straits, and ready to
seize upon any rope which might offer help
in gaining safety.   The other and the larger

---

[1] Montaigne's offering had probably disappeared before the shrine was pillaged by the French, as there is
no mention of it in a catalogue of the *ex votos* by Murri,
printed in 1792.

In 1802 Eustace visited Loreto and found the treasury
empty. "No vestige now remains of this celebrated
collection of everything that was valuable; rows of
empty shelves and numberless cases only enable the
treasurer to enlarge on its immensity and curse the
banditti that plundered it. 'Galli,' he adds, 'semper
rapaces, crudeles, barbarorum omnium Italis infestissimi.'"
—*Classical Tour*, i. 166.

portion of the cottage serves as a chapel,
but no daylight finds its way thereinto, and
the altar is placed beneath the grating and
against the partition already alluded to.   In
it neither ornaments, nor benches, nor chairs,
nor paintings, nor wall-hangings are to be
found, for it is itself a shrine. No swords
or arms of any sort may be taken therein,
and no respect is paid to a man because of
his high rank. We partook of the Eucha-
rist there, a privilege not granted to all, as
another chapel is provided for this function
on account of the vast crowds of people
who commonly present themselves.   So
great is the throng every day in this chapel
that it is necessary to be there in good
time to find standing room. When I com-
municated a German Jesuit said mass.
People are forbidden to pare off bits of the
masonry; indeed were they permitted to
carry away aught of the same the whole
fabric would disappear in three days. They
tell of innumerable miracles in relation to
the place, for details of which I refer the

reader to the books dealing with the same, but many have happened in recent times; also for an account of the mishaps which have befallen those who, out of devotion, have abstracted fragments of the building, even with the Pope's warrant. Also they show a little bit of brick which had been taken away while the Council of Trent was sitting, and was brought back by miraculous agency. The cottage itself has been cased outside and strengthened by a square fabric of the most sumptuous character made of the finest marble and carved all over.[1] Few rarer or more exquisite works can be seen elsewhere. Around and above this structure is a large and beautiful church with many fine chapels and tombs, amongst which is that of the Cardinal d'Amboise,[2] which

[1] The marble casing of the Santa Casa was designed by Bramante and the sculptures executed by Sansovino, Girolamo Lombardo, Bandinelli, Giovanni da Bologna, Guglielmo della Porta, Raffaele da Montelupo, Sangallo, and others. It was begun under Leo X. and finished under Paul III.

[2] Louis d'Amboise was born in 1479, and made cardinal by Julius II. He died at Ancona in 1517.

the cardinal of Armaignac [1] caused to be erected. The cottage itself serves as the choir of this church, which, however, has a choir of its own, but this is set in a corner. The whole of this great church is covered with pictures, frescoes, and painted legends, [2] and we saw therein divers rich ornamental gifts, but I was surprised not to find more, considering how ancient is the fame of this church. I have a suspicion that they melt down the old silver plate and put it to other purposes; in any case it is estimated that their annual offerings amount to ten thousand crowns of coined money. No other place I have ever visited makes so great a show of religion. All property

[1] Georges d'Armagnac was born in Gascony in 1500, and became a Spanish ecclesiastic. He subsequently was made archbishop of Toulouse, and died at Avignon in 1585.

[2] The principal works now in the church are by Luca Signorelli, and Melozzo da Forli. Montaigne does not notice the bronze doors by Girolamo Lombardo, which rival Ghiberti's at Florence. The church was begun in 1468 on the site of an ancient one which, according to Vasari, was adorned with frescoes by Domenico Veneziano and his pupil Piero della Francesca.

which is lost there—and I speak of articles
of silver or others not only worth picking
up, but worth appropriating by people thus
inclined—is deposited by the finders in a
certain public receptacle provided for the
purpose. Any one who may be so minded
may abstract whatsoever he may desire from
this receptacle without any cognisance being
taken thereof. When I was there I saw
many articles thus displayed, paternosters,
handkerchiefs, and purses, such as none
would own, all at the disposal of the first
claimant. With regard to such things as
you may buy and leave behind you for the
sake of the church, none of the artificers
thereof will accept any payment for his
labour, for these craftsmen reckon that, by
charging only for the silver or the wood,
they themselves share the benefit of the act;
anything like almsgiving or treating they
steadily refuse. Likewise the church officials,
who are most attentive to those who wish
to confess or to partake of the communion,
and in every other respect, will accept

nothing for their services. The custom is to give to some one or other of them a sum of money to be distributed amongst the poor in your name after your departure. Whilst I was in the *sacrarium* there came a man who offered to the first priest he met a silver cup because of a vow he had made; and because he had vowed an offering of the value of twelve crowns, and had laid out less than this on the cup, he paid the balance on the spot to the aforesaid priest, who had put in a plea for the payment of this sum of money as the strict due of the church, and necessary for the perfect and conscientious fulfilment of the vow. When this was done the priest led the man into the *sacrarium* so that he might himself offer the cup to Our Lady and say a short prayer, the money being dropped into the common alms-box. Instances like this occur daily. Gifts are received in a very off-hand fashion, indeed the acceptance of them is reckoned a favour conferred.

I tarried the Monday, Tuesday, and Wed-

nesday morning, and went away after mass.
To declare my experience which I gathered in
this place, where I was vastly entertained and
interested, I may say that my visit coincided
with that of M. Michel Marteau, Seigneur
de la Chapelle, a rich young Parisian[1] travelling with a large following. I received from
him and from certain of his suite a careful
and detailed account of the cure of a diseased
leg, which he affirmed had been brought
about during a former visit of his to this
place, and the account given to me of this
miracle was as exact as could be. All the
surgeons of Paris and Italy had been baffled,
the patient had spent more than three thousand crowns, and his knee had been swollen,
powerless, and very painful for the last three
years. It grew worse, and more inflamed

---

[1] According to Querlon, there is no record of any such
person in the *Nomenclature alphabétique des nobles de
Paris et provinces voisines*, a list made at the end of the
sixteenth century. Neither does the Abbé Lebœuf, in
his *Histoire de la ville et du diocese de Paris*, find the
name of Marteau in connection with any one of the four
places called La Chapelle described in his book.

and red, so that he was thrown into a fever.
For several days he had ceased to use any
medicament or remedy; when, having fallen
asleep, he dreamt all of a sudden that he was
healed, and that a flash of light seemed to
shine around him.   He awoke, cried out that
he was cured, called for his servants, arose
from his bed, and began to walk for the first
time since he had been seized with this in-
firmity.   The swelling of the knee disappeared, the shrivelled and half-dead skin got
well from that time without any further
remedy.   Being now completely cured, he
had come back to Loreto, his cure having
been worked about a month earlier, while he
was here.   He had been in Rome while we
were staying there.   These were all the
authentic facts I could collect from the
discourse I had with him and with his
people.

The story of the miracle of the trans-
ference of this house, which is held to be the
actual birthplace of Jesus Christ at Nazareth,
and of its conveyance first into Sclavonia,

next to a spot close hereto, and finally to this very place, is set forth on large marble tablets fixed along the pillars of the church, and written in Italian, Sclavonic, French, German, and Spanish. In the choir I saw hanging a standard of our sovereign, the only king's device in the place. They told me that great crowds of Sclavonians are wont to come here to worship, and moreover, that as soon as they catch sight of the place from their barks at sea they set up a cry, which they let continue in the town itself, with many protestations and promises added, and beg Our Lady to return to their land, pouring out their regrets that they should have given her reason for deserting them; which thing seemed to me very marvellous.

I was told that the journey from Loreto to Naples, one I was fain to take, might be made along the sea-coast in eight easy days' travel. I should have to go by Pescara to Chieti, whence a carrier set out for Naples every Sunday. I offered money to several of the priests, but nearly all refused to accept it, and those who took it made all sorts of demur and difficulty. In Loreto they keep their grain in vaults under the streets. On the 25th of April I presented my *ex voto*. Our journey of four days and a half from Rome to Loreto cost six crowns of fifty soldi each, for the horses, for the men who let them to us and fed them, and for ourselves. This is a bad sort of bargain to make, seeing that they always hurry you along for the sake of saving their own outlay, and treat you in very niggardly fashion.

On the 26th I went to see the Port, three miles distant, which I found to be a very fine one, and a fort overlooking it which belongs to the town of Recanati. Don Luca Giovanni, the *Beneficiale*, and Giovanni Gregorio da Cailli, *Custode della Sagrestia*, gave me their names when I was leaving, so that, in case I should need their services for myself or for others, I might write to them; moreover, I received many other courteous attentions from the aforenamed. The former is in chief authority over the small shrine, and refused all the gifts I offered him. I shall always feel under obligation to them for their courtesies of word and deed.

END OF VOL. II.

Lightning Source UK Ltd.
Milton Keynes UK
26 September 2010

160398UK00001B/9/A